HOW IT FEELS
TO FIND YOURSELF

THAT WHICH SEEMS THE MOST FEEBLE
AND BEWILDERED IN YOU IS THE
STRONGEST AND MOST DETERMINED.

— Kahlil Gibran, *The Prophet*

ALSO BY MEERA LEE PATEL

• • •

My Friend Fear: Finding Magic in the Unknown

Journals

Start Where You Are: A Journal for Self-Exploration

Made Out of Stars: A Journal for Self-Realization

Create Your Own Calm: A Journal for Quieting Anxiety

HOW IT FEELS TO FIND YOURSELF

Navigating life's changes with purpose, clarity and heart

MEERA LEE PATEL

A TarcherPerigee Book

tarcherperigee

An imprint of Penguin Random House LLC
penguinrandomhouse.com

TarcherPerigee with tp colophon is a registered trademark of Penguin Random
House LLC.

Most TarcherPerigee books are available at special quantity discounts for bulk
purchase for sales promotions, premiums, fund-raising, and educational needs.
Special books or book excerpts also can be created to fit specific needs. For details,
write: SpecialMarkets@penguinrandomhouse.com.

ISBN 9780593418734

Printed in China
10 9 8 7 6 5 4 3 2 1

Book design by Meera Lee Patel and Shannon Nicole Plunkett

FOR NADI LUNA)

hold onto yourself tightly

Contents

HOW IT FEELS TO FIND YOURSELF

Introduction

It's January 2020, and I live on a small farm in the woods north of Nashville, Tennessee, where we've been renovating our home for the past two years. The work has been difficult but rewarding for a person like me, someone conditioned to associate her self-worth with achievement. Life is full of things I can't control, but my ability to meet goals is not one of them. The harder I work, the better I feel about myself, confident that I'm earning my place in this world.

The city girl in me learns how to cut and lay tile, install trim, insulate walls, and seal windows. My husband tills the soil and plants seeds; in turn, I harvest more vegetables than I know what to do with. Our shelves are lined with canned pickles and sweet and savory preserves, and our freezer is stuffed with zucchini breads, summer squash tarts, and dozens of fresh tomato sauces. This is my winter preparation.

Now it is winter, and the weather is icy and gray. It has been for months. I'm newly pregnant with my first child, a welcome surprise. I'm excited for the transition awaiting me—eager to step into a new role and determined to excel. I want to become somebody entirely new. Somebody better. Everything is about to change.

By April, there is no semblance of the world I lived in a few months ago. The pandemic enveloped the entire country in confusion and panic before splitting it in two. On the farm, we are safely quarantined, months away from understanding the true impact of never-ending isolation. We order groceries online and disinfect them on the steps before bringing them inside. It's impossible to find flour, beans, or fresh produce, and what we do find arrives rotted and moldy. We rely on our preserves, understanding how lucky we are to have access to food, our home, and each other. For so many, there is nowhere to go and no one to ask for help.

I am in month four of my pregnancy. I wake each morning hoping it'll be the last day of nausea, not knowing the sickness will carry well into my final trimester. The excitement I felt a few months ago has dissipated, leaving a cycle of anxiety in its place. Shadows of doubt begin to follow me, reminding me of all I don't know—and that day by day, I'm losing the little time I have left to figure it out.

I don't know how to be a mother. I still turn to my own parents for all sorts of advice, ranging from practical to philosophical: *How do you rewire an electrical outlet? What removes rust stains? Yes, I am grateful for what I have, but sometimes I feel guilty for having it—don't you?* Although there's plenty we don't agree on, I find value in their insights and lived experiences. When it comes to myself, I feel less certain. I grow older each year, yet I still don't feel that sure—really, of anything. I don't know how to love another person completely or teach them to love themselves. I'm not very patient or understanding—two shortcomings that I'm confident will complicate parenthood. What is it like to be responsible for a child? How do I balance work and motherhood, and how will I transition from who I am to who I need to become? I worry about my identity constantly, consumed by the fear of becoming someone I no longer recognize.

Everything has changed. I'm stuck in between—no longer who I used to be, and no closer to the person I wanted to be by now. I don't know how to navigate this moment, this stretch of time that feels so unbearably uncertain. I don't want to make the wrong choice. Where do I go from here?

———

There's a collective obsession with achievement in Western society—the harmful notion that reaching a desired destination is more valuable than the path it took to get there. I've often wished I could skip ahead past this messy middle, but the gratifying moments in life, the ones we remember long after they pass, are found in transition: in the gritty periods between where we are now and where we choose to go next.

If you want a life filled with purpose and meaning, skipping ahead is not an option. What is? Navigating these transitions thoughtfully, by making decisions that align with your core values. At the foundation of this practice is self-exploration, which requires you to have conversations with yourself. This sounds simple but can feel overwhelming, especially when your time and attention are already stretched thin.

When I began my own journey, I used concrete actions to help me consciously engage with myself. I paid close attention to how I moved through the world by diligently asking myself questions and writing down the answers. I challenged my own feelings and impulses. I engaged in vulnerable conversations with people I trusted, sharing more of myself with the hope that they'd eventually feel comfortable doing the same. I peeled away years of conditioning and inherited truths to discover what it was that I, as an independently thinking and feeling adult, truly believed.

The past few years have turned much of what we knew about our lives upside down. The pandemic that swept through my life swept through yours, too, leaving us both without any sense of normalcy or routine. We've lost loved ones over the phone, unable to help or hold them, often without saying goodbye at all. Some friendships have disappeared with distance or politics; some have bloomed with strength and surprise. Our children have grown up inside our homes, without classrooms or classmates. We've changed jobs and homes, moved on or away. We've been stuck, unable to mourn or celebrate the moments in our lives. We hold on to our health and hope with gratitude as best we can. We are displaced, many of us in multiple ways, and we've become isolated—from ourselves and one another.

It's through moments of great change, of overwhelming upheaval, that we begin to discover ourselves. Our culture expects immediate solutions for difficult situations, but the ever-changing nature of life doesn't provide any of those—and neither does this book. This book doesn't offer topical inspiration or positive thinking as a doorway to permanent happiness, neither of which is healthy nor possible. Navigating life's painful periods with resilience and kindness—for yourself and for others—builds tenacity, confidence, and empathy. Your endurance grows, as does your ability to accept even the most difficult experiences in life.

I am not interested in perpetual happiness. I want to embrace the entire spectrum of human emotion, to find value in every experience that wraps itself around me. Within these pages, I share moments from my own life and the broader lessons I've learned, attempting to answer the universally persistent question responsible for shaping my personal values, self-understanding, and capacity for growth: *How can I keep going?*

As an artist, I tend to think and feel in color. Assigning colors to my emotions allows me to identify each one, helping me understand what I'm feeling, when I'm feeling it. After some time has passed, I find it easier to extract meaning from each experience. Understanding how you best process your experiences is foundational to your self-exploration practice. I encourage you to journal, exercise, or meditate—to engage in the practices that bring you clarity.

The color palettes in this book distill fundamental life transitions and explore the processes of moving through them with presence. The short essays that accompany them are a collection of memories, emotional snapshots, and reflective exercises that have encouraged growth, critical thought, and significant shifts within me. The palettes and stories I share in these pages aren't full of simple answers. They may not always point you in one direction. Rather, I hope they encourage you to see your own life as a beautiful, complex rainbow, full of meaning in moments of joy and satisfaction—but also within the painful experiences of change, loss, and growth. This book asks you to be responsible for yourself and your choices. It asks you to do the challenging work of examining yourself. When you know yourself well, it's easier to locate the significance in every small moment. Your capacity to retain peace during difficult transitions increases. You understand that most situations have more than one correct answer. You feel freer.

The most important relationship we can spend our lives nurturing is the relationship we have with ourselves. The lens through which we view ourselves determines our connection to the world. If that lens is cracked or cloudy, each of our relationships begins to suffer. Building a strong internal compass that skillfully guides you through life's uncertainties is possible only by developing an intimate, healthy relationship with yourself. Through this process of continued self-exploration, I began to learn who I am, what my purpose is, and how to intentionally shape my life into one I recognize with joy. Living well means adapting to life's constant transition; evolving with purpose and clarity is a skill I now practice regularly. This is how I found myself—for the first time, and then again, every time after that.

● ● ●

FINDING
MYSELF

WHO AM I?

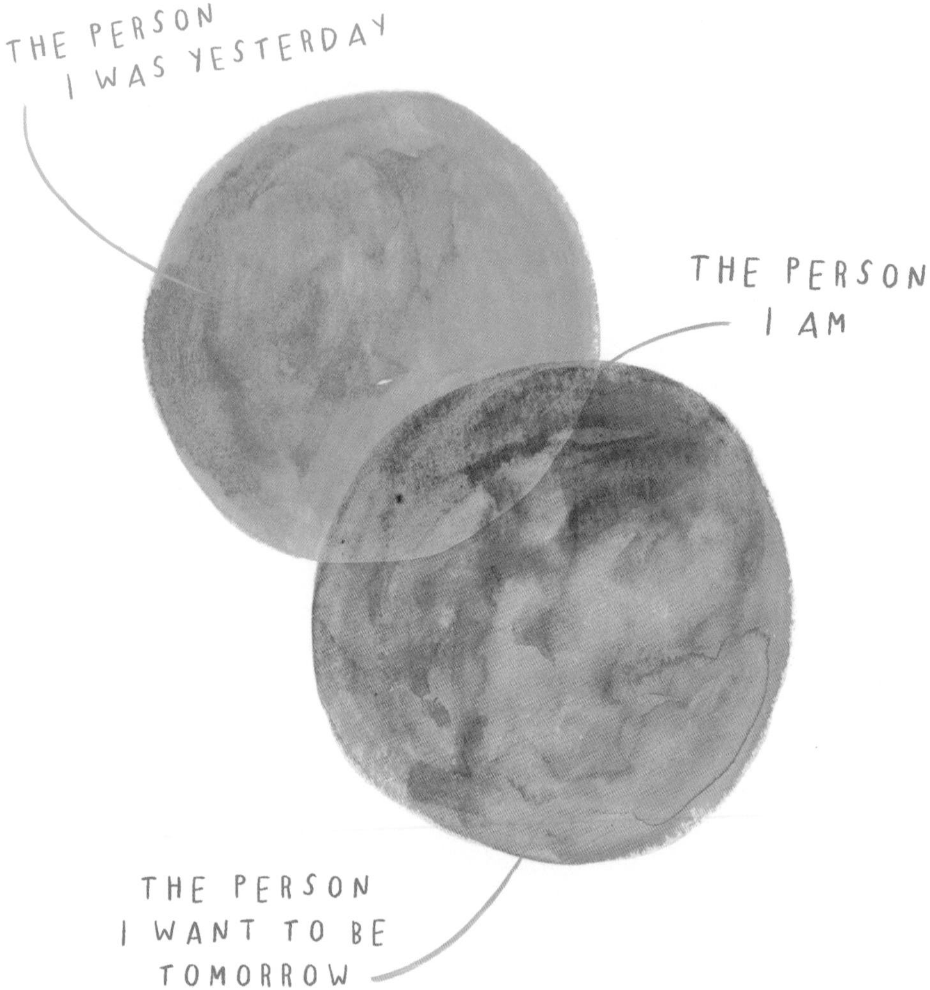

THE PERSON
I WAS YESTERDAY

THE PERSON
I AM

THE PERSON
I WANT TO BE
TOMORROW

Self-exploration is an admittance of responsibility: it requires you to accept the consequences of your thoughts and behavior. Examining your values and exploring why you think and feel in certain ways builds confidence and self-assurance, which helps you make deliberate choices that reflect who you are and hope to become.

After years of having an open dialogue with myself and consciously spending time following my curiosity, I began, very slowly, to recognize myself. My reflection changed from a trembling outline to a solid shape, complete with colors, textures, and detail. It feels good to know myself—to understand the emotions and reactions that stir within me and to recognize my thought patterns and impulses.

Moments of FAILURE lead to TRANSFORMATIVE GROWtH.

I learned that stability isn't a steady job or someone to come home to every night. It's the knowledge that no matter what thunderstorms rumble outside my window, my self-reliance won't be shaken. Fortifying my self-reliance has given me the resilience to welcome change when it inevitably appears.

No one has themselves fully figured out—you are ever-changing, which means that understanding who you are will be a continual process, too. Go at your own pace. Don't be afraid to stumble or fall; moments of failure lead to transformative growth. The path toward self-recognition is one you'll walk on your entire life—and there's no better way to spend your time.

● ● ●

WHEN I'M STUCK
IN A CYCLE OF ANXIETY

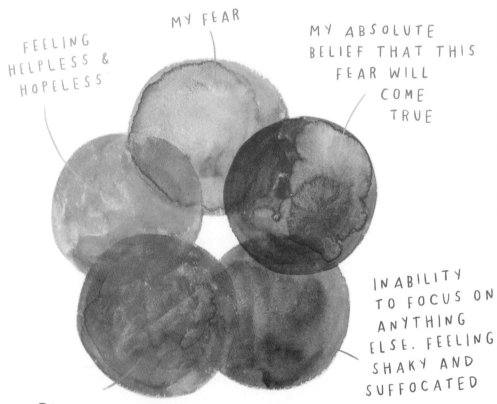

FEELING HELPLESS & HOPELESS

MY FEAR

MY ABSOLUTE BELIEF THAT THIS FEAR WILL COME TRUE

INABILITY TO FOCUS ON ANYTHING ELSE. FEELING SHAKY AND SUFFOCATED

THINGS WILL NEVER BE OK AGAIN

When I feel anxious, I try to shift my focus from what I can't control to what I can: my own thoughts and actions. *I am responsible for my own happiness* is a reminder I repeat to myself regularly. These words reinforce the belief that how I feel is up to me; no one else can poison my happiness or well-being unless I let them. This mindset shift puts me back in control, easing any panic beginning to creep in. If I'm already anxious, I address it rather than ignore it out of shame or insecurity—especially because naming anxiety is one of the quickest ways to deflate it.

Through years of experimentation, I've learned which actions quiet my anxiety. I meditate, walk outdoors, and journal to help balance myself and maintain a healthy perspective. It's not easy, or always possible, to engage in these practices during stressful periods. Instead of reprimanding myself for falling short, I give myself permission to simply begin again— whenever I feel ready to do so.

I AM RESPONSIBLE FOR MY OWN happiness.

• • •

WHAT IT'S LIKE
TO FEEL LOST

ME

(DOESN'T KNOW
WHAT TO DO)

EVERYONE ELSE

(HAS IT FIGURED OUT)

*I*solation is the hardest part of feeling lost. We keep feelings of confusion to ourselves because we assume that everyone else knows what they're doing. The first time I confessed to a friend I trusted that I felt lost, I was surprised by her honest response: she, too, often doesn't know what to do next. The truth is that most of us wake up each day and navigate the best we can, without a map or lantern to guide us. It's impossible to know *how* to do something *before* you've done it, and most of life is spent navigating the unknown.

Sharing my confusion removes the shame I feel, erasing the belief that I should always know exactly where I'm going—and that it's a failure if I don't. Each day, I take a step forward in the direction I believe is best. If it proves to be the wrong path, as it often does, I summon the courage to change course and try again. Instead of asking myself to carry the burden of infallibility, all I ask of myself is that I try, the best I can, to keep going.

Sharing my CONFUSION removes the shame I feel.

• • •

WHEN I TRY TO CHANGE THE WAY MY BRAIN WORKS

IDENTIFY WHAT TO CHANGE

SLOWLY FORGE NEW PATHWAYS IN BRAIN

GATHER DETERMINATION AND TAKE ACTION

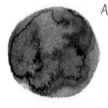

PICK MYSELF BACK UP. TRY AGAIN.

SLIP BACK INTO OLD HABITS

BEAT MYSELF UP FOR FAILING

When I was twenty-eight, I decided I was going to be an unfailingly hopeful person. Instead of harboring cynical thoughts, I wanted to see the brighter side of things. I wanted to believe that anything was possible.

The trouble was that my cynicism kept creeping in like kudzu, no matter how hard I tried to uproot it. I'd have a day or two where I brushed away negative thoughts, but by day three, I'd find myself slipping back into old patterns of thinking. I'd become so disappointed in myself that I'd give up, believing I was incapable of genuine change.

Our brains are made up of neural pathways that become stronger with use. The more we engage in a particular behavior or pattern of thinking, the deeper that neural pathway becomes. To change our existing habits, we must build new pathways and use them consistently until they become automatic. Understanding this helped me become more patient with myself. I realized that slipping up doesn't mean giving up—rather, it's an opportunity to try again. Each time I consciously rewire my brain by engaging an encouraging mindset rather than a cynical one, I become a bit more hopeful—in myself and in my ability to change.

● ● ●

HOW TO STOP FEELING GUILTY ABOUT NOT BEING PRODUCTIVE

STOP COMPARING YOURSELF TO ANYONE ELSE. IT'S GUARANTEED HEARTACHE.

RE-EVALUATE WHAT "PRODUCTIVE" MEANS. TAKING CARE OF YOURSELF & OTHERS IS OF THE GREATEST VALUE.

DISCONNECT YOUR SELF-WORTH FROM ANY ACHIEVEMENTS. SELF-WORTH COMES FROM WITHIN, IT'S NOT SOMETHING YOU EARN.

FOCUS ON WHAT'S IN FRONT OF YOU, NOT ON WHAT YOU COULD OR SHOULD BE DOING.

LIFE IS A PROCESS, NOT A RACE. ENJOY WHERE YOU ARE NOW.

REMEMBER THAT TIME IS PRECIOUS. SPEND MORE OF IT ENJOYING THE SIMPLE WONDER OF BEING.

We live in a time when we are painfully aware of what others are accomplishing, and it's often a constant reminder of what we're not. When you feel guilty for not working—for relaxing, pursuing hobbies, or simply feeling content—ask yourself the following questions.

- **What is the source of your self-worth?** My insecurity is at its highest when my self-worth is linked to something outside myself: career success or achievements. I feel guilty if I haven't worked a certain number of hours, because I believe my worth is intrinsically linked to my productivity. I believe I must *earn* my value as a human being.

- **What if that source disappears?** There is always the possibility of losing your job, being unable to pursue your goals for, say, health reasons, or simply being unable to meet your own expectations. Ensuring that your self-worth is internally rooted is necessary for enjoying yourself and your life, guilt-free.

- **What do you value about yourself?** For me, it is my discipline, my thoughtfulness, and my ability to empathize with others and help them feel seen. Valuing myself for existing as a unique being in the world allows me to seek validation and self-worth from myself, rather than from others.

Society is designed to feed off our output; feeling content despite my fluctuating productivity is a continuous work in progress. I regularly remind myself of my inherent value, finding that when I do, I no longer need to frantically goal-seek to feel worthy.

●　○　●

WHAT IT FEELS LIKE
TO BE STUCK IN BETWEEN

WHERE
I WAS

WHERE
I WANT
TO BE

THE PLACE
I CAN'T SEEM
TO GET OUT OF

The in-between is a temporary space we all find ourselves in when the place we were in has disappeared and the road ahead isn't yet clear. When I'm stuck in the in-between for too long, it's because I'm scared to venture ahead, into the unknown. What am I afraid of? Falling short and proving my own ineptitude to myself. And although feeling stuck isn't fun, it certainly feels safer than failure. In these moments, remembering my own capability is the easiest way to reclaim agency over my life—because believing I can do something helps me do it.

Make a list of all the difficulties you've overcome and the lessons each experience has taught you. What have you learned? How have you changed? What unexpected strength came to you when you least expected it, and where did you find it?

I keep this reminder close: *My speed is not as important as my dedication to inner growth.* There is no beauty in a perfect, linear life. There is beauty in challenge, adversity, and failure—and in the very places of confusion that feel too intimidating to wade through. There is beauty in bravery, in venturing uncertainly into the unknown. There is beauty in each step you take, in creating strength, determination, and new beginnings from the places you were once too scared to leave.

There is NO BEAUTY in a perfect, linear life.

• • •

THE PROCESS OF LOVING MYSELF

RESPECT MYSELF
BY SETTING BOUNDARIES

SPEND TIME WITH
MYSELF. EXPLORE
WHY I THINK
AND FEEL THE
WAY I DO.

CULTIVATE
PRIDE AND JOY
WITHIN MYSELF,
FOR MYSELF

SPEND TIME WITH
PEOPLE WHO HELP ME
FEEL MORE LIKE
MYSELF,
DOING THINGS THAT
HELP ME FEEL FREE

SEE MYSELF
AS A PERSON
WORTHY OF LOVE

CARE FOR MYSELF
THE WAY I WOULD A
FRIEND OR LOVED

I've always approached myself self-critically: by identifying where I fall short, I'm able to see where I can improve. Years of self-criticism, however, made it difficult for me to love or forgive myself. When I decided to work on loving myself, I began with self-acceptance. Accepting myself helped me resist myself less, which reduced the number of internal battles I fought each day. When I listened to myself, my self-trust and intuition awakened, which meant I relied less on the approval of others. The validation I valued most came from myself.

Learning how to love myself required me to change my thought patterns. Instead of thinking, *I don't like myself,* I made a list of all the qualities I loved about myself. Instead of thinking, *I'm too weird to be loved. No one will understand me,* I asked myself, *Am I so different that I won't be loved? Am I so unusual that no one else will understand me?* Changing the way my mind processed internal criticism prevented me from entering an irrational thought cycle. I made efforts to understand myself better by asking myself questions and accepting the answers without judgment. Accepting myself has made it easier to love others, also with less judgment. Loving myself makes it possible for me to receive love from others and feel the love that has always surrounded me.

• • •

WHEN YOU FEEL YOURSELF CHANGING

A CURIOSITY,
A LONGING—
WANTING
MORE.

THE SELF—AWARENESS
NEEDED TO SEE THAT
CHANGE IS
NECESSARY.

PATIENCE &
RESOLVE.
MAKING A
COMMITMENT TO
BE GENTLE WITH
YOURSELF.

TAKING SMALL,
INCREMENTAL
STEPS FORWARD.
BEING DELIBERATE
WITH YOUR HEART.

ALLOWING OTHERS
IN. REMEMBERING
THAT YOU ARE
NEVER AS ALONE
AS YOU MAY FEEL.

THE RELIABLE
PASSAGE OF
TIME.

Change is prickly, especially when you're not sure in what direction you're headed. It's confusing to no longer align with ideas or choices that used to make sense, or to feel like an outsider within the community you've been a part of for so long. In several moments throughout my life, I've consciously examined the social circles I was a part of, realizing that I felt detachment instead of community. This was troubling. It was like living among strangers, where no matter how hard I tried, I couldn't quite let down my guard enough to be myself.

Our emotions often reflect the onset of change before our minds do. It took time for my brain to string together these seemingly random feelings into a clearer picture that I could understand. As a person, I'd changed, and despite my greatest efforts, I no longer felt understood by my existing community. My priorities had shifted, and what I needed from a friendship had, too. When you feel resistance toward something or someone you've always loved, it's usually an indication of growth. Be patient with yourself. Become familiar with the feelings that are arising. Spend time exploring new friendships and interests, and remain open to a life that looks different from the one you'd imagined—one that more closely aligns with the values you have now. Remaining fluid ensures that life will surprise you in unexpected, beautiful ways.

RESISTANCE IS AN INDICATION OF GROWTH.

• • •

HOW I FEEL AFTER
A GOOD NIGHT'S SLEEP

WILLING TO
TRY SOMETHING
NEW

GROUNDED
PERSPECTIVE

PEACEFUL

LIKE EVERYTHING
IS POSSIBLE

CONFIDENT

CAPABLE OF
ANYTHING

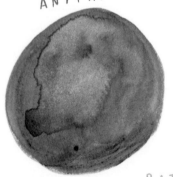

30 SECONDS
AWAY FROM BREAKING
INTO SONG

RATIONAL

*I*n a world that values productivity over health, it's easy for sleep to be the priority we sacrifice most willingly. We believe we're invincible and that our education, careers, or children are worth neglecting our minds and bodies for. The reality is that when your relationship with sleep suffers, every other relationship you value does, too. Sleep is one of the most vital nutrients our brains need to think clearly and make rational decisions, to feel emotionally balanced, and to maintain a healthy perspective.

Doctors and therapists will tell you it's never a smart idea to make an important life decision when you are sleep deprived. Instead, focus on clearing your mind, eating a healthy meal, and getting a good night's rest. When I have trouble winding down before bed, I meditate for fifteen to twenty minutes (using an app or simple deep breathing exercises) and journal to empty the anxious thoughts cycling in my mind. Sticking to a sleep schedule has made this easier: I wake up and go to bed at the same time each day and don't use my phone or computer for an hour before bed or for an hour after waking up. These simple changes help me sleep better, which means the way I think and feel improves, too. Usually, I'll find that even high-stress situations feel a bit more manageable in the morning.

• • •

HOW TO LET GO
OF SELF-DOUBT

ERASE IMPOSTER SYNDROME: THE
BELIEF THAT I DON'T DESERVE
OR HAVEN'T EARNED MY SUCCESS.

LISTEN TO MY FEAR: WHAT GREAT
DREAM AM I AFRAID OF PURSUING?

WHAT AM I MORE AFRAID OF: NEVER
REACHING MY DREAM OR NOT EVEN
GIVING MYSELF THE CHANCE TO TRY?

TAKE ACTION: UNDERSTAND
THAT EACH STEP FORWARD
BUILDS CONFIDENCE.

From time to time, I'll realize that I'm living a smaller life than I want. I usually blame this on my partner, my family, my job responsibilities, my environment—anything other than myself. The reason I feel this way isn't because of any external factors, however. It's because of the mental boundaries I've built that prevent me from believing another life is possible. I'm worried about or frightened by things that haven't happened yet, and likely never will. I keep myself from growing because I'm too concerned someone else won't like who I've become. I feel like an absolute imposter walking around in my own life, pretending that I know how to be an artist, a mother, a friend.

Working through self-doubt enables me to live a bigger life. How do I do this? I listen to my fear when it tells me what I want most. Self-doubt is the fear of failure, and the fear of failure indicates that

Self-doubt is the fear of FAILURE.

I have an important dream that requires my time and attention. In fact, this dream is so important to me that the idea of trying to achieve it—and failing—seems worse than ignoring it altogether. In moments of self-doubt and fear, I ask myself: *Should I keep myself from moving toward this dream because I'm afraid of failing? Or is keeping myself from trying the greatest failure of all?*

● ● ●

WHEN YOU BECOME WHOLE ON YOUR OWN

KNOWING YOURSELF CLEARLY.
SHAPING YOURSELF ACCORDING
TO YOUR OWN VALUES, NOT
SOMEONE ELSE'S.

RECOGNIZING
THAT YOU ARE
RESPONSIBLE
FOR YOUR OWN
HAPPINESS
AND NO
ONE ELSE'S.

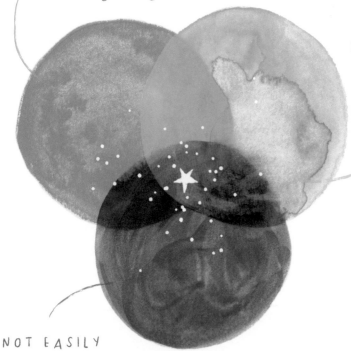

NOT EASILY
DETERRED, HAVING
REALIZED THAT YOU CAN
DEPEND ON YOUR OWN
DETERMINATION TO TAKE
YOU ANYWHERE.

I spent most of my twenties waiting for someone else to put me together: to tell me I was good enough, to make me less afraid, to teach me what I should value most. I weighed other people's opinions more than my own due to insecurity and a lack of self-trust, which meant the decisions I made were based on someone else's ideas of who I should be.

What I most longed for was a sense of wholeness, but I looked for it in the wrong place: somewhere outside myself. My life began coming together when I realized that the only person responsible for my happiness . . . is me. I stopped waiting for someone else to give me permission and began living the life I wanted. I traveled alone because I wanted to see the world. I painted because I felt there was an artist inside me. I reached out to strangers and asked if they wanted to spend time together. I nurtured these new connections and received the gift of incredible friendship in return. I said yes to opportunities that scared me and became more confident each time I accomplished something I never thought I would.

Becoming whole is an ongoing process—something you will achieve only to find that once again, it's all come undone. Life stretches to accommodate your vision of it, and what I dreamt of was a life bursting with a variety of experiences and environments. My life now reflects the one I dreamt of: not one without failure or sadness, but one that has a sense of fullness—because there is meaning stitched through every experience.

LIFE STRETCHES TO ACCOMMODATE YOUR VISION OF IT.

● ● ●

FINDING
MYSELF

FINDING
LOVE

WHAT LOVE LOOKS LIKE

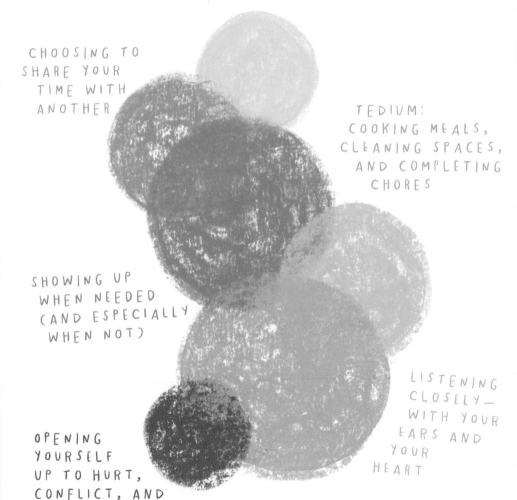

ENCOURAGING
A LOVED ONE
TO REST

CHOOSING TO
SHARE YOUR
TIME WITH
ANOTHER

TEDIUM:
COOKING MEALS,
CLEANING SPACES,
AND COMPLETING
CHORES

SHOWING UP
WHEN NEEDED
(AND ESPECIALLY
WHEN NOT)

LISTENING
CLOSELY—
WITH YOUR
EARS AND
YOUR
HEART

OPENING
YOURSELF
UP TO HURT,
CONFLICT, AND
CHALLENGE

*T*he amount of work was unimaginable. Four years' worth of furniture, tools, animal feed, and hay sat in the shed waiting to be sorted, sold, or cleared out. The basement was full of boxes—many of which we hadn't even gotten a chance to unpack yet.

And then there was the rest of the house—the kitchen with the large walk-in pantry and bulk stores of flour and grain, cast-iron pots and pans, fingerprinted cookbooks, and wilting potted plants. The bedrooms with their furniture, linens, and more books than we had time to read. Our chickens, in need of a new home. The greenhouse, the orchard, the garden beds, the tiny house—an entire farm to prune and sell, a new home to find and move into.

All this and a six-month-old, two full-time working parents, a book that needed writing—and graduate school beginning in less than two months. All this and knee-deep, still, in a pandemic that seemed to stretch on and on, meaning no one could come help. But you did. You quarantined and then you came to pack our boxes. You wrapped furniture in blankets and cleaned the floors. You scraped tile and scrubbed windows. This is what love looks like: your hands blistered and paint-stained, loading the truck and then my car. Your ears listening to my worries late into the night. Your eyes seeing my stress and then taking me in both arms. This is what love looks like. I know because you showed me.

● ○ ●

THE THINGS ABOUT LOVE THAT SCARE ME

VULNERABILITY: What if my fears and insecurities are used against me?

DEPENDENCY: On another person for validation, comfort, joy

LOVE'S MIRROR: Seeing what I don't like about myself reflected back to me

THE WORK: What if I can't provide the effort and time necessary to cultivate genuine love?

*T*he people I love most are subject to the hardest sides of me—a truth that is difficult for me to accept. Slowly building the trust and intimacy needed for a meaningful relationship requires me to be vulnerable and to possess the compassion that allows another person to feel safe sharing themselves with me. This means letting others see the pieces of me that are stricken with shame and resentment, the ones that are angry and misunderstood, the ones that are confused or unable to move on. It also means understanding that I may not receive the reaction I'm seeking, whether that's comfort, validation, or advice. Another person's reaction is not within my control.

Despite knowing they care for me, there's a tiny voice of caution warning me to keep up my guard. This voice wants to keep me safe. It reminds me that vulnerability invites the opportunity for rejection and disappointment. It reminds me that there are parts of myself that I've hidden away for a reason, and that they should always remain hidden if I want anyone to love me.

I've been rejected for sharing my true self many times. As hurtful as it was, the rejection was never about me—it was about the person who pushed me away. A person who is unable to respect my vulnerability is not the right person to share it with and not the relationship I want to invest my time in. My truth isn't too sharp or difficult to sit with; it's simply more than some people can, or want, to carry. That is their choice. My choice is to remain open, knowing deep amounts of vulnerability are necessary for the meaningful relationships I'd like to build.

● ● ●

THE FIRST TIME YOU'RE EMOTIONALLY VULNERABLE WITH SOMEONE

FEAR, FEELING
UTTERLY EXPOSED

RISK OF
BEING REJECTED

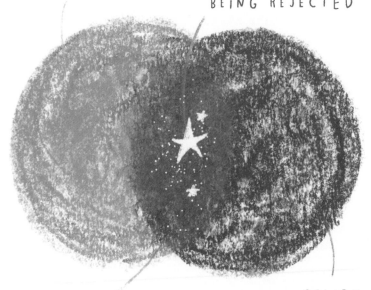

INTIMACY &
CONNECTION

RELIEF AND
PEACE THAT
ACCOMPANIES
HONESTY

There is a thought that I keep close to my heart and consider often: *There are so many beautiful things waiting for me on the other side of my fear.* I am careful to welcome new people and experiences, despite the chance of rejection, because just as likely is the chance that my vulnerability will introduce me to a brighter world—one where I feel comfortable being fully seen and understood.

I've built up resilience against rejection, knowing that if someone is incapable of accepting my honesty, it's because they are engaged in a battle against themselves, not against me. Vulnerability creates a renewable energy—each time I open myself up, I am encouraged by how this simple act can bring me closer to someone else. When I give another person the chance to see me, I also give myself the opportunity to love myself more. The wins are worth the wounds. Each time I share a part of myself and see the hint of recognition in someone else's eyes, I see myself, again, for the very first time.

There are so many BEAUTIFUL things WAITING FOR me on the other side of my fear.

● ● ●

HOW LOVE FEELS
IN THE BEGINNING

TINGLY,
EFFERVESCENT,
REFRESHING

FULL OF PROMISE
AND POSSIBILITY

SERENDIPITOUS:
OVERLAPS IN
MEMORY,
INTERESTS,
EXPERIENCES,
UNDERSTANDINGS.

A GIANT SURPRISE:
MYSTERIOUS AND
UNCERTAIN. A RISK
I WANTED TO TAKE.

SELFLESS: A STRONG
DESIRE TO BECOME BETTER
FOR SOMEONE ELSE.

I swiped right without really thinking. Online dating is like that: overwhelming due to the infinite pool of available matches, exhausting for the same reasons. We sent a few messages back and forth, and when that quickly became tiresome, we agreed to meet at the local park for a walk.

I felt curious, which was new. In the six months since I'd last been on a date, my life had completely changed. I'd prioritized my own happiness, and in return, I'd developed a tranquil contentment. I was open. I felt satisfied. Needing to impress another person felt like a foreign idea.

It was a sunny day in Nashville, hot but not far enough into May to feel sticky. There were birds and a welcome breeze and greenery that dazzled, stretching on for miles. The park was a former airport, and the tarmac led to a densely wooded hiking trail. As we headed toward it, I thought about first date safety and pulled my bag closer to my body. He joked about it then. He still jokes about it today.

Everything we spoke about carried significance: our past relationships, our values, and what we wanted in our futures. The conversation was natural, easy. We laughed often. I felt light, in the way that's possible only with someone you've known for a long time.

He was a stranger. Instead of feeling skeptical, I savored the refreshment that our intimate conversation offered. If this didn't lead anywhere—even if I never saw him again—I knew this walk was worth the swipe.

● ● ●

WHAT TO DO WHEN YOU FEEL UNSURE

LISTEN TO
YOUR HEART

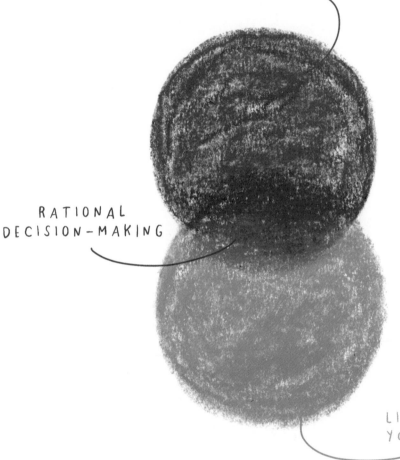

RATIONAL
DECISION-MAKING

LISTEN TO
YOUR HEAD

Confusion breeds when our internal compasses are jammed—they don't know enough about what we want or need to point us in the correct direction. Uncertainty is born from two failures: not asking yourself enough questions (neglecting your head) and not paying attention to how your body feels (neglecting your heart).

Questions to ask your head are:

- Does this person renew my energy or deplete it?
- Is our relationship mutual? Am I giving more than I'm receiving?
- Do I feel positively challenged by our friendship? Does this person encourage my personal growth or prohibit it?
- Do we have shared values? Do we respect each other?

Questions to ask your heart are:

- How does my body feel around this person? Do they bring me peace or anxiety?
- Do I feel more or less like myself around them? Are they asking me to be someone I'm not?
- Am I ignoring any red flags? Does this person make me feel uncomfortable or uneasy in any way?
- Is our time together easy, or do I have to mentally prepare myself for it?

Answering these simple questions aligns my head with my heart, leading to clearer thoughts. I regularly work on overcoming the desire to change another person under the disguise of helping them. The only person I can change is myself, and the only people I can help are the ones who ask for it. Some relationships are forever, some are for now, and some are simply better left behind.

WHEN YOU TRY TO CHANGE WHO YOU ARE FOR SOMEONE ELSE

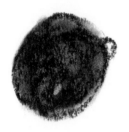

SHAME.

It becomes difficult to look at yourself when you don't recognize the person in the mirror.

UNCERTAINTY.

Will this even work? Is someone else's acceptance worth abandoning who you are?

GUILT.

Betraying the person that's always been there for you: you.

CONFUSION.

There's someone else's voice in your head, and it becomes harder to recognize your own.

*A*s social beings, we want validation: to know that others desire our presence in their lives. We want to believe we matter. Each time I've tried to change myself to please someone else, I failed. When I dated someone who felt I was too fiery, I made myself smaller, letting my opinions and thoughts collect in my throat. I became timid. I found that I was disappointed in who I had become, and when that disappointment became too great an ocean to remain afloat in, I finally walked away.

Healthy, long-lasting change only occurs when the desire for change comes from within, with the intention of becoming more closely aligned to the person you want to be. There is plenty I work on changing about myself, but my intensity, strength, and wit—traits I admire about myself, although they are challenging for others—are not on that list.

When I'm tempted to mold myself into a person I think other people will like more, I ask myself the following questions:

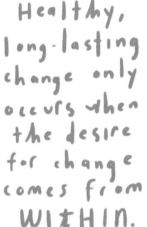

Healthy, long-lasting change only occurs when the desire for change comes from WITHIN.

- Is someone asking me to change for them or for my own well-being?

- Is this trait or habit harmful to myself or others?

- Does this change align with my personal values? If so, how?

● ● ●

WHAT AN UNHEALTHY RELATIONSHIP FEELS LIKE

DISORIENTING.
No longer knowing if my thoughts and feelings are rational.

GASLIGHTING.
Manipulated to feel that my reality is fictional, my boundaries unwarranted.

INVISIBILITY.
The hesitation to show or express myself. Feeling unseen, unheard.

UNCERTAINTY.
Continually unsure of where our relationship stands or whether we're on the same page.

What I remember most is how hopeless it felt to consider the future, to imagine a different life. What I remember most is how I felt comfortable letting anyone other than you see me. What I remember most is having to conceal my joy from you. What I remember most is having to defend you to others, and especially to myself. What I remember most is the constant anxiety, the what-ifs, and the wonderings. What I remember most is the lack of trust. What I remember most is the confusion, the bewilderment, the disbelief that a person could behave this way.

If I could go back, I'd tell myself not to settle. If I could go back, I'd tell myself that I deserve more. If I could go back, I'd tell myself that helping you shouldn't require me to hurt myself. If I could go back, I'd tell myself not to change, especially for someone who doesn't know who they are or what they want.

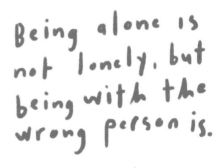

Being alone is not lonely, but being with the wrong person is.

If I could go back, I'd tell myself that being alone is not lonely, but being with the wrong person is. If I could go back, I'd tell myself how freeing it is to simply walk away.

● ● ●

WHAT IT FEELS LIKE TO FALL APART

DENIAL. This isn't happening. How did things unravel so quickly?

SMALL BITS OF HOPE. Morning sunlight on your face. A cool breeze on your walk to work.

EMOTIONAL PAIN THAT MANIFESTS PHYSICALLY. When your heart hurts, your b body absorbs the pain.

A NEW BEGINNING. The idea that things can be different, maybe even good, again.

BARGAINING. Promising the world that you'll become a better or different version of yourself if only things would change.

ACCEPTANCE. Knowing that although you can't change the past, the future is entirely up to you.

CONVICTION. The genuine belief that you will never be known and loved again.

When I was fifteen, I began engaging in what I now know to be my life-long struggle with depression. Recognizing that the most difficult relationship in my life would be the one I have with myself was devastating, especially at such a young, tumultuous age. I didn't understand why I didn't like myself. I didn't understand why I woke up wishing to be in someone else's body, wanting to swap my brain for one with a different set of thoughts.

Although I now know there were several, slow-burning disconnections responsible for my depression, at the time, it felt like a light switch: one day I was fine, and the next, I'd unraveled. I made a lot of promises to the earth, vowing to try harder and be kinder, to have more gratitude if the feelings of hopelessness and self-loathing would dissipate.

Every relationship changes. Just as my depression developed over time, my ability to love and accept myself began gradually, slowly deepening with each passing day. I am continuously learning how to love myself better and to deepen my capacity to hold that love. Some days are harder than others. There are days when I feel my heart harden and begin to close. But then the leaves rustle and fall with the help of a passing wind, and I'm reminded that no feeling is final—and this, too, shall pass.

No FEELING IS FINAL— and this, too, shall pass.

● ● ●

HOW I KNEW THIS TIME
WAS DIFFERENT

I ALWAYS
FELT LIKE
MYSELF

NEVER FELT
ALONE IN THEIR
PRESENCE

NO ITCHINESS
OR DESPERATION

TRUST: HEALTHY
INTENTIONS PAIRED
WITH SUPPORTING
ACTIONS

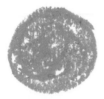

NO NEED
FOR CONSTANT
ANALYSIS

ALIGNED
VALUES

knew it was different because there was space for me—room for me to grow and learn without the expectation of becoming someone else. I knew it was different because there was an absence of toxicity. There was no incessant tugging on my heart, no cautionary voice warning me to turn around. I knew it was different because I never felt like I was in the wrong story, trying to fit into a place where I didn't belong. I knew it was different because my body didn't shut down. I didn't feel irritated or itchy, eager to get away.

I knew it was different because I recognized the ways his presence nourished me. I didn't feel whole—only I can make myself whole—but I was softened, soothed in worn areas. I knew it was different because I felt accepted. I didn't always feel understood, but I was still supported. I was encouraged to become a healthier version of myself, to grow into the person I'd like to be. I knew it was different because I didn't feel dependent. Instead, I felt the simple desire to share: my time, friendship, and mind.

I knew it was different because there was room for me... to grow.

• • •

HOW TO FIGHT FAIRLY

SHOCK. How could they possibly feel this way?

ANGER.
The accumulation of tiny grievances melting into one hot rage.

THE FIRST RECONSIDERATION
Maybe this relationship is not what I want.

MISCOMMUNICATION.
Hearing words that were never said, saying something you wish you hadn't.

THE SECOND RECONSIDERATION.
Maybe this is an opportunity to grow closer

EVENTUAL CALM.
A commitment to keep doing The Work, and to keep communicating.

My husband and I bought a small farm north of Nashville, Tennessee, six months after we met, embarking on a journey to grow our own food, while renovating our home, together. I'd recently quit my job, leaving my home of Brooklyn, New York, in pursuit of change. To say that I experienced culture shock is an understatement. My body held on to this stress, burying it deep within my cells. When it finally made its way out of my body, it looked a lot like my husband and me standing barefoot in the hallway of our new home having a stunning shouting match about who felt the most wronged.

It isn't easy to share a life with another person. Pairing up two people with different histories and expecting them to avoid any sort of conflict is unreasonable. Not only is fighting normal, it's necessary—it's a relationship's way of uncovering wounds so they can heal.

When I'm overcome with emotion, these boundaries help me fight fairly:

- Reminding myself that vulnerability is sacred, grounded in trust. I don't use my partner's insecurities, secrets, or past mistakes against them.

- Using "I" statements ("I feel hurt that . . .") helps me take responsibility for my feelings and actions instead of placing blame on my partner.

- Reminding myself that we're on the same team, working toward a shared goal: a healthy, connected partnership.

● ● ●

WHAT LOVING MYSELF TEACHES ME

THERE IS NO
ROMANCE IN
MARTYRDOM

HOW TO
ALLOW
OTHERS
TO LOVE ME

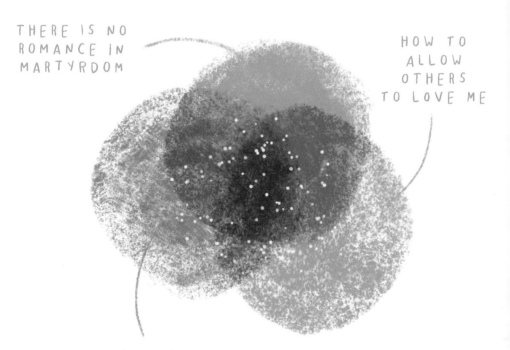

ALL I NEED
IS WITHIN ME
(SUPPORT, LOVE,
VALIDATION, JOY)

It's April 2019, and I'm getting married. I expected to feel frenetic, nervous about the unknown place I was stepping into.

Instead, I feel steady. This growth, this transition into a new chapter, has been happening for a long time. It's been happening for my whole life—each time I identify a fear freezing me still and move forward *because* of it. My fear teaches me that being in places of discomfort is where I learn the most about myself.

When I'm afraid of rejection, I choose to accept myself. When I feel lonely or isolated, I ask myself why. In myself, I've found the things I've always looked for in someone else: a friend, a good listener, a person who understands and empathizes. Loving myself has been an integral part of learning to love another—and learning to let myself be loved. When I didn't love myself, it was impossible to feel anyone else's love for me.

So often we believe we must wait for something else to change before we can: the calendar year, the seasons, the night to melt into day. We wait because we don't want to live in discomfort. We wait because we don't want to make big changes alone. We wait to feel ready, not knowing that confidence builds after we begin.

What I wanted most was to find someone who understood me, but along the way, I realized that all I've ever needed was the patience to understand myself—and to love the person I am.

● ● ●

WHAT LOVE
ACTUALLY FEELS LIKE

EFFORT &
PATIENCE

GROWTH &
EVOLUTION

HEARING &
SEEING

UNDERSTANDING

COMMUNICATION

RESPECT
& VALUE

SELF-
BETTERMENT

CAPACITY TO
SERVE YOURSELF
& THOSE YOU
LOVE

TRUST &
INTIMACY

TIME

*I*n the handful of years since I met my partner, love has looked vastly different. Love has been winding walks to nowhere, small tokens of affection (hand-drawn maps and notebook poems), and listening to Charles Bradley records while lying on the living room floor. It's experiencing different languages and cultures together, two-day plane rides, and slowly overlapping our separate worlds into a Venn diagram. Love is maintaining our individuality while nurturing our relationship.

During the last two years, while navigating pregnancy and birth during the pandemic, love has looked like patience and perseverance. It's giving each other our uncompromised attention after long, never-ending months of working and parenting without breaks. Love is looking at each other instead of at our phones. It's taking care of each other so we can take care of ourselves, like T putting the baby to bed so I can do my physical therapy exercises before I get too tired. Love is laughing whenever we can, and especially when life feels overwhelming and impossible. It is remembering how lucky we are to have each other.

Genuine love isn't found; it's fostered. Many people consider this version of love—the kind that asks us to be responsible with each other's hearts—disappointing or stale. For me, it's hard to think of something more exciting than understanding the complicated, intricate inner workings of someone I love. With each passing day, we become new people. There is so much to discover about each other—and there always will be.

● ● ●

WHAT AN OPEN HEART
HAS SHOWN ME

THAT THE WORLD,
AND EVERYTHING IN IT,
CAN SURPRISE AND
DELIGHT ME IF
I LET IT

CONVICTION CAN
OFTEN FORCE ME TO
MISS LIFE'S MOST
BEAUTIFUL
MOMENTS

MY IDEAS
OF WHAT
WILL MAKE
ME HAPPY
ARE OFTEN
INCORRECT

I HAVE
THE
STRENGTH
TO ENDURE

THE
IMPORTANCE
OF BOUNDARIES

MY CAPACITY
FOR GROWTH
IS ENDLESS

The clouds are in fine form today, puffs of thick white acrylic smears. Occasionally, the sun pierces through. I don't see the birds as I shuffle along with my head down, but I listen to their music. Morning walks are like this: the sky bobbing over me while I retreat further into myself. We moved to St. Louis, Missouri, in June. It's October now, and I haven't made a single friend.

I turn the stroller onto Des Peres and navigate the cracked sidewalk toward the playground. Up ahead is a young woman with her baby. I slow down, hoping she'll leave before I get closer. No such luck.

"Hello! Do you live nearby?" she asks me. My heart turns clockwise, tightening.

"Yes," I say politely. "Just down the street." I unstrap N and watch her toddle over to the slide. I feel resistant. I've met many people in this city, but none I connected with. I'm tired of trying.

My heart spins, quietly reminding me that it is there. *There are many people to love*, it says, *but you have stopped looking for them*.

The children play together. I ask the woman questions and listen intently to her voice. I engage my curiosity, studying her face: her long eyelashes and curly hair, the way her eyes crinkle when she smiles, her soft laugh. She looks at N with the love only a mother can feel for a stranger's child. Opening your heart is like learning a foreign language—it feels self-conscious and clumsy until it doesn't.

Stepping outside yourself: that's what an open heart is. A story that invites you to first look and then listen. A morning at the playground, an unexpected conversation, smears of cloud, a tiny hand in mine.

• • •

FINDING
MYSELF

FINDING
LOVE

FINDING
FRIENDSHIP

DIFFERENT TYPES
OF FRIENDSHIPS

The one who
understands
without
explanation

The one that
challenges you

THE ONE WHO
SEES YOU CLEARER
THAN YOU SEE
YOURSELF

THE ONE THAT
DOESN'T MAKE
SENSE

The one where
we go months
without speaking
(and nothing
changes)

THE ONE THAT
SPARKED AND
FIZZLED OUT

The one you
cultivated
by choice

The one
you've had
since
childhood

THE ONE YOU'RE
SURE YOU KNEW
LIFETIMES AGO

THE ONE THAT
BECAME SO MUCH
MORE THAN YOU
EXPECTED

THE ONE YOU KNOW WON'T
LAST, BUT IN THIS MOMENT
IS SWEET

I have friends I connect with deeply, who understand my spirit and philosophies, but who don't understand the intricacies of being a self-employed artist, which is a very big part of who I am. I have friends who are also working parents and empathize with constant split attention and inconsistent childcare, but who don't understand me creatively. I have a creative cohort that carries me through deadlines and writer's block, but who don't understand the difficulties of working while parenting during a pandemic. And then there are the rare gems: the friends who overlap with you in several ways, or who understand you completely, despite significant dissimilarities.

It's impossible for a single person to fulfill all our needs. Realizing this makes it possible to accept a friend for who they are, and what they're able to offer, rather than resenting them for who they aren't. It places less pressure on the relationship, allowing it a chance to bloom naturally rather than from a place of expectation. It's only from this place that I can appreciate how beautiful and complex my friendships are—and how lucky I am to have them.

IT'S IMPOSSIBLE FOR A SINGLE PERSON TO FULFILL ALL OUR NEEDS.

● ● ●

WHAT IT'S LIKE TO MAKE A NEW FRIEND

THE EXCITEMENT OF FORGING A NEW CONNECTION

THE HESITATION OF OPENING UP TO SOMEONE NEW

What if they don't like me? What if I don't like them?

TIPTOEING AROUND SENSITIVE SUBJECTS, POKING THE BOUNDARIES OF COMFORT

THE MOMENT OF VULNERABILITY (also the moment of truth)

A. THE EASE OF GENUINE CONNECTION

B. THE DISAPPOINTMENT IN REALIZING YOU'LL LIKELY GO YOUR SEPARATE WAYS

Cultivating the resilience to remain open, finding the courage to try again

I connected with L immediately. We were both new to Nashville, eager for companionship, and quick to realize we shared a dry sense of humor and a penchant for storytelling. We spent the first month of our friendship exploring our neighborhoods with wide eyes, taking road trips to neighboring cities, and sharing our childhoods. Our friendship was fun but tentative. I noticed that L didn't approach intimacy the same way I did: she skipped around its edges while I wanted to dive right in. If friendship was a garden, she collected seeds (the more, the better), while I loyally tended to my existing shoots. We were a match in some ways, but in many more, we weren't.

In every friendship there is a moment of truth—when a person's vulnerability, gradually increasing in volume, eventually spills over. In our friendship, this moment arrived the day L and I sat on the phone, hundreds of miles apart. I timidly expressed disappointment over how she'd handled a conflict between us and then waited for her response. A healthy friendship isn't determined by whether you quarrel often, but by your approach toward conflict and resolution. In a mutual friendship, the intimacy of vulnerability serves as a bridge, drawing two people closer to each other. For us, it didn't. I listened to L's voice falter. It dawned on me that she didn't feel the way I did about our friendship. It was nobody's fault. Sometimes two people aren't meant to remain in each other's lives—and the ones who are find a reason to stay.

● ○ ●

WHAT IT FEELS LIKE TO LOSE A FRIEND

LEFT WONDERING:
Am I difficult to
be friends with?

Did I do
something wrong?

AN ABSENCE
IN THE SHAPE OF
THAT PERSON

A PART OF
ME GONE,
TOO

GRATITUDE
FOR WHAT
WE SHARED

The lessons,
memories, and
laughs I carry
with me
always

*F*or nearly a decade, H was the closest person to me. Childhood friends are unique in their intimacy, having stood with us during such an important, developmental period in our lives. H and I knew each other deeply. We finished each other's sentences and thoughts. We overlapped in every area of life—family, work, and creative interests were all intertwined. We had our own language, a secret portal into a shared world we'd built over time. Our friendship felt uncommon, like a treasure I had stumbled upon. No two people were as close as we were—that, I was sure of.

The friendship disintegrated in our mid-twenties. We were so reliant on each other for comfort, codependent at times, that we wouldn't allow ourselves to get close to anyone else. We shut the door on any friendship that threatened ours. This was a sign of dysfunction, but I ignored it. We fought often and knew how to hurt each other well. Separately we were changing, but our friendship didn't evolve to support the people we were becoming. The last time I spoke to H was the day I realized that nostalgia wasn't strong enough to sustain a friendship. I wasn't interested in a friendship that pigeonholed me into being a person I no longer was.

Our friendship was my coming-of-age story. H and I helped each other become who we are, but we are healthier people without each other. I think of him when a song or book or moment we shared flits through my mind, a memory so old it feels like it never existed.

● ● ●

WHEN A FRIENDSHIP LASTS

THE RICHNESS
& NOSTALGIA
OF SHARED
HISTORY

SEEING
EACH OTHER
GROW,
CHANGE,
& BECOME WHO

UNDERSTANDING
WHAT OUR
FRIENDSHIP
NEEDS

TRUST,
COMFORT,
& THE SECURITY
OF TIME

THE FREEDOM
TO BE WHO
WE ARE

A DEEP
SENSE OF
KNOWING

I climb into the car after a long day of classes, and J, who's visiting for the weekend, tells me she's brought along a bottle of Perfect Day all the way from New York, having socked it away in the airplane's belly, along with dozens of bagels.

We do the "perfect day" exercise, the one where you imagine your perfect day ten years from now. In it, I live in a house with a separate studio and a family who looks just like mine. In it, I write stories and help other people share theirs. In it, a friend comes by to hang on the porch and share in laughter. In it, I feel *good*, with a body less stressed, with a mind less stretched. In it, there is time for me.

Between J and me are nineteen years of memories. My fifteen-year-old self never imagined friendships this old, but here we are: still friends. I know time goes on, but where does it go? Time becomes the ease, I think— the natural laughter, the conversations about bodies, and babies, and home. Time becomes the tears in my throat. A swift catch when I slip on the ice. All the words we don't need to say.

We're sitting outside in the fifty-something warmish weather, the sunshine glinting in our eyes, legs draped over the porch walls. I can tell it's happening *right now*—the meaningful part of life, the part you remember years later, the part that wakes the sleeping bird in your heart.

"I'm going to remember this," I say aloud. You and me on the porch, this orange wine, this moment in time. The perfect day.

● ● ●

HOW TO BE
A BETTER FRIEND

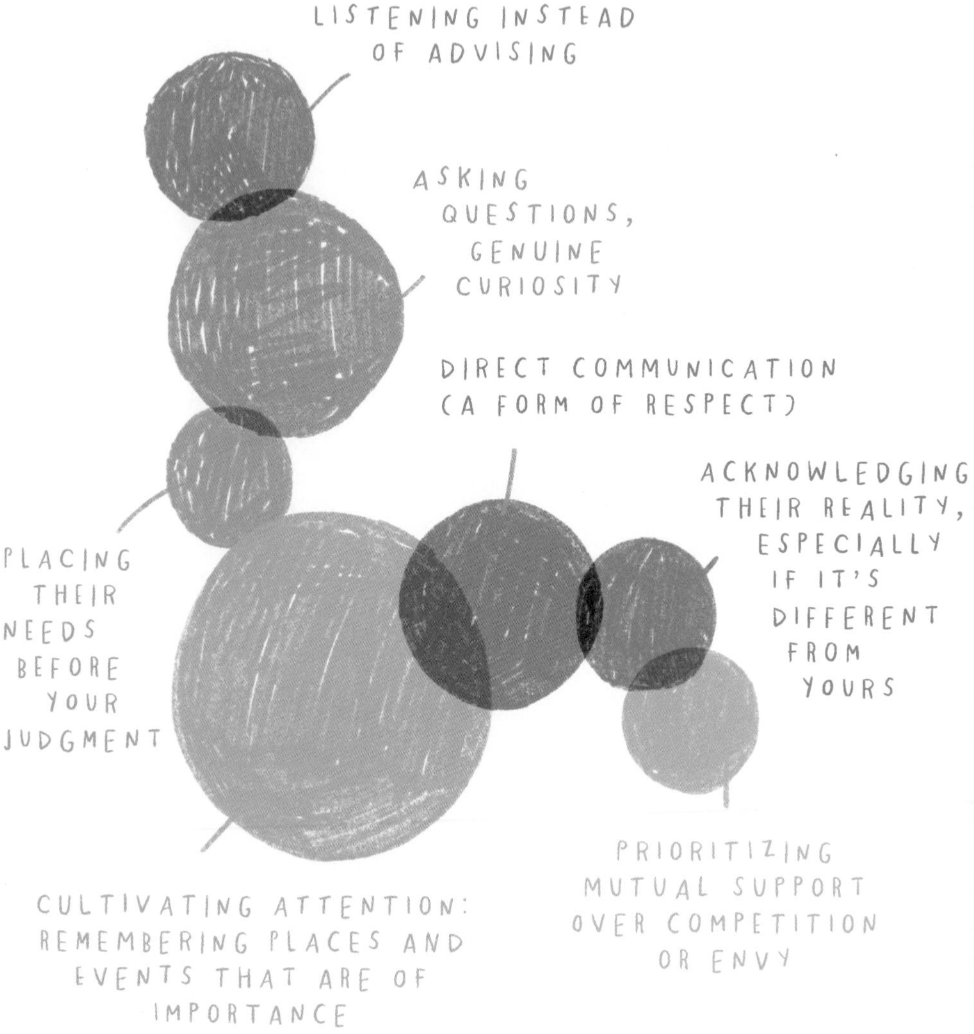

LISTENING INSTEAD
OF ADVISING

ASKING
QUESTIONS,
GENUINE
CURIOSITY

DIRECT COMMUNICATION
(A FORM OF RESPECT)

ACKNOWLEDGING
THEIR REALITY,
ESPECIALLY
IF IT'S
DIFFERENT
FROM
YOURS

PLACING
THEIR
NEEDS
BEFORE
YOUR
JUDGMENT

PRIORITIZING
MUTUAL SUPPORT
OVER COMPETITION
OR ENVY

CULTIVATING ATTENTION:
REMEMBERING PLACES AND
EVENTS THAT ARE OF
IMPORTANCE

I met K in the second grade when we were eight years old. We navigated the uncertainty and horrors of middle school, high school, and college together. In our friendship, we've helped each other through numerous relationships, lived in multiple states, and traveled to other countries. We've changed immensely as individuals, which means our friendship has changed a lot, too. We've gone through periods of doubt and separation, but each time we wanted to give up on each other, we instead decided that our friendship was worth The Work. We wanted it to be healthier.

Being loved by someone gives you strength: this love trickles into you and fortifies the places that feel worn and forgotten. After twenty-six years together, K and I are experts in forgiveness—there is no longer the question of whether we will or won't remain in each other's lives. This doesn't mean we don't hurt each other; it simply means that how we handle the pain has changed. We used to let resentment build up against each other because we felt misunderstood or taken for granted. Now, when we feel hurt, we pour our energy into curiosity. We ask questions: *How do you feel? What makes you feel this way? What do you wish would happen next? How can I help?*

Loving someone takes courage. It means accepting responsibility for the role you play in that person's life—and for protecting their heart.

● ● ●

WHAT IT FEELS LIKE TO HAVE A WEEKEND TRIP WITH MY BEST FRIENDS

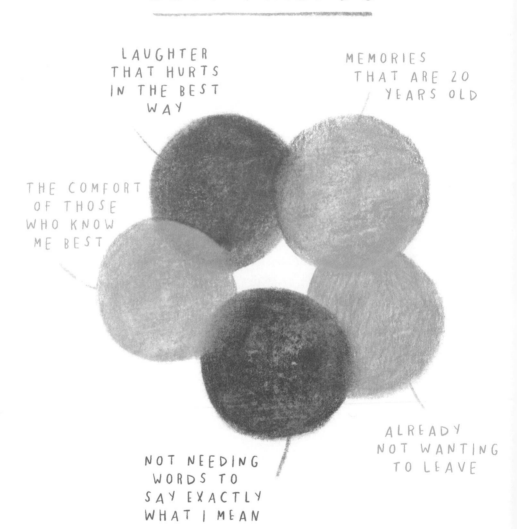

LAUGHTER THAT HURTS IN THE BEST WAY

MEMORIES THAT ARE 20 YEARS OLD

THE COMFORT OF THOSE WHO KNOW ME BEST

ALREADY NOT WANTING TO LEAVE

NOT NEEDING WORDS TO SAY EXACTLY WHAT I MEAN

*I*n the southern April heat, I pack my backpack with the items I need most. There are four pairs of clothing, most of the shirts torn or discolored and the jeans worn through in the knees. Although the teenaged version of me longed to feel womanly, as an adult, I find that the greatest gift of my unchanged body is that my wardrobe lasts a long time.

After the clothing comes my sketchbook. It is also old, the cover torn off and replaced. When I made this sketchbook, I dreamed of drawing for a living—a future I never believed would be mine. These friends I'll see soon were my support through the years of working in solitude, hoping. Wishing. I draw for a living now. Life looks so different for each of us, but our friendship goes on.

On top of the sketchbook rests my camera, a '90s Polaroid that spits out square photographs as soon as I snap them. I'm not a good photographer, but my sister is. I don't trust my memory to remember this weekend, and I know I'll want to remember. There are three of us in Utah tonight, celebrating my thirtieth birthday by hiking through Zion National Park.

I know there will be a time in the not-so-distant future when I feel alone. I take a photo so I can summon the memory of this night: watching the stars slowly emerge in the inky sky above, red rock stretching like a sleeping giant around me, the presence of two friends who have chosen me again and again. A promise to my future self that I am loved.

● ● ●

WHAT IT'S LIKE
TO FEEL KNOWN

NOT HAVING
TO EXPLAIN
HOW I FEEL

THE UNDERSTANDING
THAT COMES ONLY
FROM SHARED
EXPERIENCE

PEACEFULLY
SECURE.

THE WORDS +
GESTURES I DIDN'T
KNOW I NEEDED

VALIDATING MY
EXPERIENCE AND
FEELINGS WHEN
I'M UNABLE TO
DO SO

NEVER WORRYING
ABOUT HOW
I'M PERCEIVED

As we drive through Kentucky, I tell you about life postpartum. You can't relate, never having had a child of your own, but I feel you reaching, wanting to understand. And with so much of it, you do: the continual self-doubt, the loneliness of losing yourself, the fear that accompanies the responsibility of caring for another. I tell you about the arguments I've been having, the ones where T and I talk in circles, the ones where I feel alien, like the words coming out of my mouth are in another language—one that no one recognizes or wants to speak.

"I feel invisible," I say. "It's like I don't exist."

You don't say anything. Both of us sit in silence, but not the uncomfortable kind. I think about how each day seems to steamroll right through me. You wonder how many of my words will fall out of your mouth one day.

After a few minutes, you turn up the radio and let the hot air in through the driver's-side window. Hair flies in all directions, sticking to our faces in the sticky June humidity. We laugh and laugh until no more breath comes, listening to the wind scream all the way to my new home, a little brick number I've never even seen.

So often we reach for distractions, wanting to fill the quiet spaces in our lives. There are a few special places where silence is restorative—a balm for the aching heart—and a friendship in which you feel known is one of them.

●　●　●

THE MOMENTS THAT TURN A FRIEND INTO A FAMILY MEMBER

WHEN THE PHYSICAL
DISTANCE BETWEEN
YOU BRINGS YOU
CLOSER TOGETHER
INSTEAD OF
FARTHER APART

THE FIRST MOMENT OF
REAL VULNERABILITY
THAT MUTUALLY
BINDS YOU; THE
CONTINUED,
STEADY SHARING
OF INTIMATE MOMENTS

TAKING
CARE
OF EACH
OTHER'S
LOVED ONES

LIVING OR TRAVELING
TOGETHER; ADAPTING
TO EACH OTHER'S
NEEDS

EXPERIENCING
AN ILLNESS,
DEATH, OR
HEARTBREAK
TOGETHER

By the end of July 2020, you'd already been quarantined for four months. Jersey City, New Jersey, had gone into lockdown immediately, and you'd been teaching from your one-bedroom apartment. A week later, you tested negative for COVID-19, took a flight to North Carolina, quarantined for seven days, and then tested negative again. Your rental car was a silver Ford Fusion—small, light, and not entirely reliable. The wind tossed you around, you said. You drove for seven hours straight, not stopping for water or a restroom, fueled by fear and your own resolve. I was five months pregnant with my first child. "I wouldn't be able to live with myself if I got you sick," you said.

The sun was still hot when you arrived, wearing two masks under a face shield. You could've passed as a medic, but you were wearing gym shorts. We didn't hug until you'd showered. No one had been inside my house since February; neither of us knew what was safe anymore. You stayed for ten days, taking care of me in all the ways I needed: cooking healthy meals, cleaning the house I'd neglected, packing the freezer with homemade soups and sauces so I wouldn't have to worry about cooking when the baby came. You baked into bread the pounds of zucchini T insisted on growing, the counter stacked with loaves of all shapes and sizes. The sink overflowed with hundreds of tiny, dark green ribbons.

On Sunday, you packed your things to go home. I watched you and cried.

"Thanks for coming all this way," I said. "You went through so much to be here."

"We're family," you said. "This is where I'm supposed to be."

● ● ●

FINDING
FAMILY

FINDING
MYSELF

FINDING
LOVE

FINDING
FRIENDSHIP

WHAT IT'S LIKE TO BE THE CHILD OF IMMIGRANTS

WHO
I WANT
TO BE

WHO
I AM

WHO
THEY WANT
ME TO BE

*A*fter eight long years, I finally quit my job. I came home and cried, certain I'd just made the biggest mistake of my life. My boss thought so, too, because she'd put my resignation letter in her desk drawer instead of giving it to HR. "Take a few days and think about this," she said. "Is this really what you want? You can always be an artist on the side."

My dad didn't say much. He wasn't sure I'd made the right decision either, but he knew how life worked. The next day, he sent the whole family a one-sentence email that read: "Hurdles, mishaps, setbacks, bumps, detours, and challenges all are our teachers, and we must learn from them and move on."

I didn't go back to work. Instead, I kept making enormous life changes that scared me. I gave up my apartment in Brooklyn. I packed a backpack with only the essentials and decided to spend the rest of 2017 traveling through the United States alone. The vast openness of my own life scared me. I needed to understand my own fear.

Ten months later, I came back to New Jersey to collect my possessions. I was moving to Nashville, having met the man who would become my husband while traveling across the country. "Look at you," my dad said. "You work for yourself. You built your own business. You don't answer to anyone else; you do the work that you love. You are not afraid."

"I've stayed at the same job for thirty years. I haven't done anything else with my life. But when I was your age, I already had you and your sister, a mortgage to pay, a wife to care for. I couldn't take the risk. I wasn't strong enough to."

"But, Dad," I said. "The choices you made enabled me to pursue my dreams. I have freedom because you stayed at your job. I built a business because you taught me how to save and the importance of financial independence. I'm an artist because you taught me that happiness comes from

THE DOZENS OF YEARS THAT EXISTED BEFORE I DID, EACH ONE STAINED WITH ITS OWN HIGHS AND LOWS, LESSONS, AND MEMORIES. EACH CROSSROADS WE COME TO BRANCHES OUT IN INFINITE DIRECTIONS. THERE'S RARELY A SINGLE CORRECT PATH TOWARD ANYWHERE YOU WANT TO GO.

within—that's the reason I was able to make the decisions that shaped my life into what it is."

I could almost hear him sink into his own thoughts as we sat on the phone, listening to each other breathe. I felt the weight of everything I didn't know pushing itself between us: his childhood in Jamshedpur, India; the college years in Benares; immigrating to the United States as a young, newly married man in his twenties. The dozens of years that existed before I did, each one stained with its own highs and lows, lessons, and memories. Each crossroads we come to branches out in infinite directions. There's rarely a single correct path toward anywhere you want to go.

"Yes," he said, and then nothing more. The space between us stretched, melancholy and wide, wistful with all the lives he'd left behind.

● ○ ●

HOW A PARENT-CHILD RELATIONSHIP CHANGES

PARENT CARES
FOR CHILD

PARENT GUIDES
CHILD THROUGH
THEIR LIVED
EXPERIENCE

PARENT
TEACHES
CHILD
TO INTUIT

CHILD INTUITS
INDEPENDENTLY

CHILD LEARNS
THROUGH
THEIR OWN
EXPERIENCES

PARENT AND CHILD
BECOME PEERS

CHILD GUIDES
PARENT THROUGH
THEIR LIVED
EXPERIENCE

CHILD
CARES FOR
PARENT

*I*magine a lobster. A lobster's shell is her guardian—it protects her, houses her, and encourages her to move freely, with confidence and ease. As she grows, this shell, originally designed for protection, becomes tighter until it's simply too uncomfortable to wear. A lobster's shell doesn't have the capability to grow with her. If she wishes to survive, she must leave it behind.

We depend on our parents to keep us physically and emotionally safe from birth. They guide us the best they can, often by preventing us from making too many mistakes or experimenting with risk. As we grow older, we become people of our own—very often with different beliefs and world-views from the ones we were raised with. It becomes necessary for our relationship with our parents to change as we do.

If one or both sides never matures to see the other as individuals—as separately thinking, feeling people with their own sense of self—a peer-to-peer dynamic fails to develop. So does a genuine friendship. A parent-child friendship is unique: it's a relationship built without obligation or guilt, one in which you don't have to rely on each other, but you can, if you choose to.

It's a major source of disappointment and pain when either side refuses to let this natural evolution occur. This is a true loss; it is overwhelmingly rare and beautiful to finally befriend a parent who has loved you for so long.

● ● ●

HOW IT FEELS TO DISAPPOINT YOUR PARENTS

GUILT
FOR PUTTING
THEM THROUGH
HARDSHIP

SHAMEFULLY
ADMITTING
THAT I KNEW
BETTER

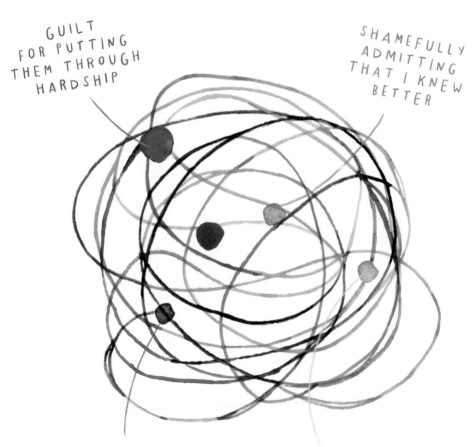

LOSS OF SELF
WHEN DISAPPOINTING
THEM MEANS DENYING
WHO I AM

TORN BETWEEN
HONORING THEM OR
HONORING MYSELF

e are raised to believe that our parents love us unconditionally. This belief shatters when you feel a breach in their love or acceptance, especially if it's caused by you making a decision they disagree with—even though it's the right one for you.

What a parent can't always say is this: *You won't always make decisions I agree with. That's OK. It's up to me to respond in a healthy way. I love you regardless of whether I agree with you or not. You don't owe anything to anyone other than yourself. It may not feel good to disappoint me, but it will feel worse to disappoint yourself. Listen to yourself. Make decisions that honor who you are.*

LISTEN TO YOURSELF.
MAKE DECISIONS THAT
HONOR WHO YOU ARE.

● ● ●

WHEN IT FEELS LIKE NO ONE IN YOUR FAMILY UNDERSTANDS YOU

AN OUTSIDER IN MY OWN HOME

LONELINESS. IF MY OWN FAMILY DOESN'T UNDERSTAND ME, OR TRY TO, WHAT'S THE LIKELIHOOD SOMEONE ELSE EVER WILL?

WANTING TO BE KNOWN

WANTING TO BE LEFT ALONE

Although we can't choose the families we're born into, we can choose how we respond to their words and behavior.

- **Approach your family with empathy.** Your parents are from a different generation, which may as well be a different planet. Like mine, they may have grown up with a different culture, in a different country. They were raised with a different set of values; many of the expectations and obstacles they faced are ones we'll never encounter. Likewise, your siblings are not you. Although you overlap in many ways, they are separate people with a distinct set of experiences and beliefs. When you disagree, ask them to explain their feelings clearly. Do your best to keep an open mind so it becomes easier to understand why they feel the way they do. Ask yourself: *If I experienced what they have, would I also feel this way? What would my behavior look like? How would I want others to approach me?*

- **Set boundaries.** You are not required to absorb anyone else's harmful feelings, opinions, and behaviors—even your family's. Establish respectful boundaries, like limiting the length of a phone call or visit, especially if doing so enables you to live a healthier, happier life.

- **Seek support elsewhere.** Not everyone has family who tries to understand them. If yours isn't interested in valuing who you are, create your own family—a community who seeks to validate and support you because they want to, not because they have to. Often, our true families aren't the ones we were born into—they are created by the people who choose to be an active, thoughtful part of our lives.

● ○ ●

WHEN YOU AND YOUR FAMILY BEGIN TO DRIFT APART

DISORIENTING. WERE THINGS ALWAYS THIS WAY?

IS OUR DYNAMIC TRULY SHIFTING OR IS IT ME THAT'S CHANGING?

HURTFUL. WHY DON'T THEY MAKE MORE OF AN EFFORT?

RELIEF. MAYBE I'LL BE FREE FROM OBLIGATORY PHONE CALLS AND VISITS.

WHERE DO I GO FROM

WHAT DO I DO NOW?

*A*s a young adult, the only family dynamic I was familiar with was my own. This made it difficult to discern whether the relationship I had with my family was healthy. I wondered: *Did other people feel like their family genuinely knew them? Did anyone else feel like they were playing the part of someone they were supposed to be? Was it normal to have a close relationship with your sibling, or was it more common to simply tolerate each other?*

As I grew older, I observed the relationship patterns within my own family as well as my friends' families. I noticed that the happiest families were those who embraced one another as individuals. They deliberately made the effort to understand one another, placing priority on clear communication and quality time together. I also realized that creating change is a team effort. It became clear that shifting the dynamic of a family is impossible to do alone: each member must be open, honest, and willing to change.

Methods for encouraging change within your own family dynamic:

- Speak honestly, even though it's hard to do so. Explain what familial patterns you'd like to change and why, and how this change will bring you closer.

- Acknowledge your own behavior. Ask your family members how you can improve your relationship with them.

Be patient, and accept that change takes time. Each small step may feel meaningless, but eventually, they will create an entirely new path.

● ● ●

THINGS I WISH I COULD SAY TO MY PARENTS

I'm working very hard to unlearn what you've taught me

I WISH YOU WEREN'T HURTING THIS WAY

I DON'T NEED YOU TO DO THIS FOR ME

It's unhelpful when you assume you know better than me

YOU'D BE HAPPIER & HEALTHIER IF...

I don't fully feel I can be myself around you

I DON'T WANT TO PARENT MY CHILDREN THE WAY YOU PARENTED ME

I WISH YOU'D PLAY YOUR ROLE AS A PARENT SO I DON'T HAVE TO

When approaching a difficult topic of conversation with my parents, I consider the following:

- Is it important to discuss this with them, and if so, why?

- Where does my hesitation lie? Am I worried about their reaction?

- What do I want from this conversation? Am I seeking their approval or guidance? Do I hope to change their minds?

- Can I remain calm if the conversation becomes strained?

There are things I choose not to share with my parents for my own emotional self-preservation. After years of persistent attempts, there are certain topics I no longer believe are useful to discuss. Open communication is one of the most valuable characteristics in any sustainable relationship, but so are healthy boundaries.

Yet the more vulnerable I've allowed myself to be with my parents, the more open they've been with me, resulting in a fluid relationship in which we freely share and confront each other. We don't always understand each other's perspectives, and we rarely agree, but for the most part, we respect each other's individuality. I've increased my capacity for empathy through curiosity; the more questions I ask them, the better I'm able to understand them—and this lends me an even greater understanding of my childhood and how I became the person I am.

● ● ●

A LESSON IN UNCONDITIONAL LOVE

MY DESIRE
TO LOVE
UNCONDITIONALLY

A WET
NOSE

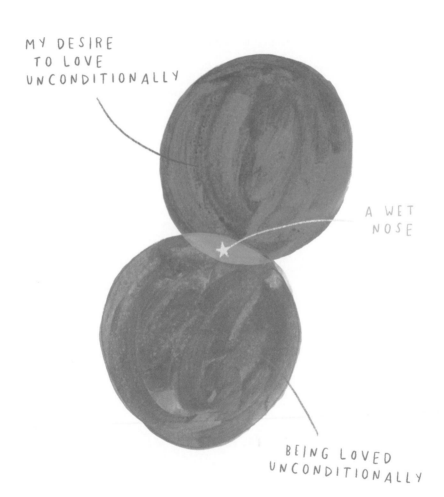

BEING LOVED
UNCONDITIONALLY

I wake up tired. It's 4:35 a.m., and our five-month-old is crying. I sit up, swing my legs over to the edge of the bed, and stumble toward the door. Jack has been up for some time now, waiting for us to wake. He dances around my feet, tip-tapping excitedly, wanting me to sit down and play with him. "I need a minute, Jackie," I mumble, stepping over him and into the bathroom. He watches as I brush my teeth and splash cold water on my face. I feel irritated for no reason. After a few minutes, I close the door.

By 6 a.m., the baby has been changed and fed and cried a few more times. We're sitting on the floor playing peekaboo, waiting for the sun to show her face. Jack sits by the bedroom door, waiting. Every so often, he looks over to see how we're doing.

Around 6:45, I get dressed. Jack bounces around my heels as I pull on pants and a hoodie. "Jack. Jackie. I need some space," I say, more gently than I have before. When we reach the back door, he's there, waiting. I let him out, and he races around the yard, joyfully feeling the cool air on his face. The trees are dropping their leaves now, and the crinkle of each one he steps on fills my ears. The scent of morning dew after a long fall from the sky passes over us in waves. I breathe in deeply and will myself into feeling new. I want to be better—patient, kind, more appreciative of all the good I have. Jack walks over and sits down next to me, so closely that his body is on my feet. His head rests under my hands. He waits.

● ● ●

WHAT IT FEELS LIKE TO CARE FOR MY PARENTS

THE
DISCOMFORT
OF THEIR
VULNERABILITY

CLUMSY. Am I
doing this right?
Do they feel safe
and cared for?

FRUSTRATING.
They don't want
my help or believe
that they need it.

STRESSFUL.
Strained under the
weight of caring for
yourself, your
family, and your
parents, too.

THE STARK AWARENESS
OF SUCH A LARGE ROLE
REVERSAL AND WHAT
IT MEANS FOR THE
FUTURE

AN OPPORTUNITY
FOR GREATER
UNDERSTANDING

At some point in our lives, we stop seeing our parents solely as our caregivers and more as individuals—people like us, with their own collection of dreams, disappointments, anxieties, and needs. We enter a gray area, an in-between place where consideration for our parents begins to affect the decisions we make.

It's impossible to prepare for this transition because you don't know when it will happen—for some of us, it happens at an early age, and for others, it happens much later in life. When you find yourself in this gray area, take some time to acknowledge and accept this change:

- **A new vulnerability.** Feeling concerned for your parents can unearth insecurities you didn't know you had, like the uncertainty of knowing whether you're giving them good advice or taking their feelings into consideration. It's OK if this feels strange—you're learning to care for someone new, and the best way to learn is by doing.

- **Ask more questions.** What makes your parents feel seen or heard? Do they want advice or someone to listen? What makes them feel reassured? How do they process pain or sadness?

- **Practice patience.** It may be difficult for you to offer your parents support. At the same time, it takes humility and strength for them to ask for—and accept—your help.

- **An opportunity for intimacy.** Often, caring for your parents feels like a stress—especially when you have your own family, work, and responsibilities to tend to, or if your relationship with them is strained. See this transition as an opportunity to know your parents more intimately—and possibly change the relationship you have with them.

● ◐ ●

THINGS I'VE INHERITED
FROM MY PARENTS

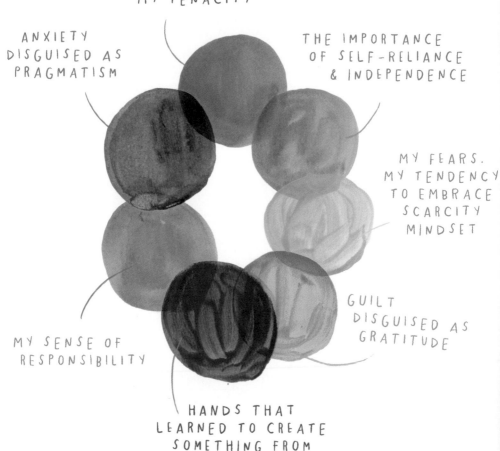

MY WORK ETHIC,
MY DILIGENCE,
MY TENACITY

ANXIETY
DISGUISED AS
PRAGMATISM

THE IMPORTANCE
OF SELF-RELIANCE
& INDEPENDENCE

MY FEARS.
MY TENDENCY
TO EMBRACE
SCARCITY
MINDSET

GUILT
DISGUISED AS
GRATITUDE

MY SENSE OF
RESPONSIBILITY

HANDS THAT
LEARNED TO CREATE
SOMETHING FROM
NOTHING

*I*t is one of the many paradoxes of life that we spend much of our adult years unlearning what we've absorbed as children. Wherever you are in your process of undoing, it may be helpful to ask yourself the following:

- What am I most afraid of?
    - Is this my fear, or was it given to me by a parent?
    - Does this fear protect me or prohibit me from living a fuller life?
    - Do I want to continue carrying this fear?

- What unhealthy habits do I see in my parents?
    - Have I adopted any of these habits?
    - What steps can I take to undo them?

- What healthy habits do I see in my parents?
    - How can I introduce these into my routine?

- Am I holding on to someone else's idea of who I should be that's preventing me from being who I am?

● ● ●

WHAT IT'S LIKE TO BE RESPONSIBLE FOR A CHILD

Hyper aware —
of my shortcomings,
agitations, and
lack of patience

THE WEIGHT OF
KNOWING THEIR
SURVIVAL
DEPENDS
ON ME

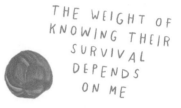

IMPOSTER SYNDROME —
I FEEL UNEDUCATED +
INEXPERIENCED, LIKE
I'M PLAYING A ROLE I
DIDN'T PREPARE FOR

Humbling.
Living within a
perpetual state of
uncertainty,
continually
learning

WANTING, SO BADLY,
TO BE SOMEONE THEY ARE
PROUD TO KNOW + BE
SHAPED BY

A distinctive bonding
experience — no other
parent has my exact
experience, but they have
their own challenges and
moments of small
triumph that
bind us

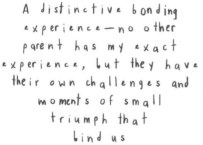

NOT WANTING TO BE
THE SOURCE OF MY
CHILD'S UNLEARNING,
WHILE ACCEPTING
THAT I INEVITABLY
WILL BE

My daughter comes into the world, and we both learn how to nurse, how to stretch, how to put ourselves back to sleep. *I don't know what I'm doing*, I think to myself each time I soothe her. It's hard for me to see past this moment in time—how can I know what things will be like before they actually are?

Each morning, she wakes with a smile. We sit on the floor, and she immediately begins to explore the carpet beneath her. Some fibers are blue, and some are magenta or green. I name each color as she touches it and wonder if I'm teaching her correctly. I'm a writer, but words feel clumsy in my mouth. What language do I use? I wonder if she prefers quiet in the morning, whether she'd rather enjoy the magic of color in silence. I don't know, so I talk aloud. "Hi, baby. I don't know what I'm doing. How can I help you find the beauty in each day? I want you to feel confident." She looks at me quizzically, not knowing what self-doubt is. She examines each fiber, rolling strands between her fingers or grabbing them in clumps. The carpet is soft and colorful. The morning light is orange, mysterious. Already the day is beautiful.

My daughter learns to roll, then crawl, then quickly begins pulling herself up. I see the determination in her eyes, the way her forehead wrinkles as she grasps on to my legs for balance. She falls quickly, and hard. For a moment she is confused, but she hasn't yet learned how to doubt herself. She tries again. Up and down, up and down. She doesn't know what she's doing, but each time she falls, she clambers back up. Her little feet aren't sure they can balance the rest of her body, but they're learning how to.

I don't know what I'm doing, and nearly everything I do manage to accomplish feels foreign and unsteady. I am trying, though. And each day I wake up and try again.

●　●　●

HOW IT FEELS
WHEN MY CHILD CAN'T
TELL ME WHAT'S WRONG

HELPLESS:
I want to ease
her struggle but
I don't know how

Wishing she
could build
strength and
resilience without
this experience

GOOGLING
EVERY POSSIBLE
QUESTION AND
SCENARIO

THE DEVASTATING
REALITY OF PARENTING:
knowing there's a limit
to how much I can
provide or protect

LEARNING TO
TRUST HER
INTUITION &
HER BODY'S
NATURAL
ABILITY TO
CARE FOR HER

Trusting that
I've instilled the
right values in
her, so she can
navigate each
experience in a
healthy way

When my daughter is six months old, she gets sick for the first time in her young life. She's drinking milk and then suddenly, she's not—she's vomiting. Vomit splatters everywhere: on the pillows, on the sheets, on the floor. It drips down the bedroom wall and pools near my slippers. The baby sputters and wails, confused and gasping for breath. There is an uproar somewhere inside her body, and she doesn't understand what's happening. Neither do I.

I've never had a sick child before. I want to take her to the pediatrician, but I don't want to expose her to something worse. Besides the hospital where she was born and this house, she's never been inside another building before. I worry about her dehydrating, so I give her more milk, but again, it comes up. "What do you need?" I ask her, so badly wanting direction. Her large, watery eyes plead for me to have an answer, to know how to make it better.

Her fever is low, so I try not to panic. I remove her congestion using a tiny infant's tube, and rub salve on her small chest and smaller feet. I hold her little body so close to mine that I can feel the tiny drum of her heartbeat. *Healing requires patience*, I tell myself. *Maybe time is the only medicine I can give her.*

"I'm here," I say while her tired eyelids flutter and she struggles to breathe. "I'm here," I say, my heart beating wildly, not knowing when it will be different. "I'm here," I repeat to myself, even after she finally falls asleep. I still need to know, to feel the air going in and out of my own lungs. *I'm here, I'm here, I'm here.*

● ● ●

THINGS I TALK
TO MY CHILD ABOUT

THE MORNING
LIGHT AS IT
CRAWLS THROUGH
OUR WINDOWS

THE FEELING A
BREEZE BRINGS;
THE SMELL OF
COLD AGAINST
OUR FACES

THE SECRET
LIVES OF
ANIMALS,
BIRDS,
& INSECTS

WHAT
HAPPENS
WHEN WE
SLEEP

THAT BEING
PATIENT IS
NOT EASY

HOW
NO ONE
REALLY
KNOWS

*I*n the morning, she watches me wake. I rub my eyes and yawn while she waits to be taken out of her crib. "What did you dream about?" I ask her, searching her face for an answer. Her sleep sack is rumpled and worn, but her smile is bright and her eyes wide. I think about how I could use a little more sleep. She thinks about how fascinating the world is.

We go out onto the porch and watch things sway in the wind. "What a beautiful breeze we're having," I say while she watches headlights cut through the darkness. The sky slowly lightens, and she studies each car or bus that passes by with growing interest. The bees are already hard at work. We watch them gather pollen from each hydrangea in the front yard and carry it elsewhere, to some unknown flower on another part of the street. "Maybe they're traveling to another neighborhood," we muse. "Maybe they're heading back to their home hive in another county. Every living thing is on its own journey."

The August sun streams in from the east, the light climbing higher and higher. It sparkles between branches and dances through the leaves. She reaches for the light and tries to pinch beams between her pointer finger and thumb. "It's strange, isn't it, how we can feel the sunlight's warmth but can't hold it in our hands?" She doesn't answer me but grasps at the rays flowing onto the porch, millions of tiny dust fragments spinning like ballerinas on a cement-and-stone stage.

● ○ ●

WHAT IT'S LIKE TO CHOOSE MY OWN FAMILY

THE DEEPEST WELL OF GRATITUDE.

The knowledge of knowing these people care for me because they want to.

AN ENTIRE SKY OF THE LUCKIEST STARS

LOVING MYSELF ENOUGH to recognize unbalanced relationships, and choosing to hold on to only those that make my life more meaningful.

A MARVEL.

Looking at my chosen family and seeing how beautifully strange its shape and color are. Seeing the difference in each person and the perspective only they could ever bring to my world.

A wore an oversized gray sweater and torn jeans, her long hair pulled back into a topknot. We'd been meeting at this coffee shop on a near-daily basis, sometimes even by chance—the beauty of living in a big city with tiny streets. It was late September, and a chill was already settling in, coating our neighborhood with the feeling of impending doom. Winter in New York always felt this way.

We discussed hotel theory. Hotel theory states that each of our lives is a hotel, and we don't have a choice over who checks in and who checks out—all we can do is take care of those who've checked in, for however long they choose to stay.

This theory has guided me through the confusion of many friendships. It's helped me focus on those who show up for me, rather than dwelling on those who don't, and encourages me to treasure our time together. The ethereal nature of friendship used to disappoint me, but now I marvel at each human being's capacity for change. Most important, hotel theory created a boundary between me and the emptiness I carry inside. This emptiness is led by a persistent desire to belong. By practicing hotel theory, I no longer seek entry into particular friend groups, reserving my energy instead for the friendships in front of me—those who have already decided I am worthy of their time, efforts, and love.

In the seven years since A first explained hotel theory to me, many people have come into my life. Most have left, but a few have remained. They've been with me through heartaches, mental illness, physical maladies, and cross-country moves. They've been there for birthday celebrations, holiday gatherings, cold morning walks, and hours around a backyard fire. I no longer wonder about our friendship dissipating. I don't take their friendship for granted because I know what incredible, irreplaceable wisdom they bring to my life. These few have become my family. We choose each other over and over again.

● ○ ●

FINDING
HOME

FINDING
FAMILY

FINDING
MYSELF

FINDING
LOVE

FINDING
FRIENDSHIP

WHAT HOME FEELS LIKE

FAMILIAR &
NOSTALGIC, LINED
WITH THE INSULATION
OF MEMORIES

EARLY MORNING
LIGHT, SURROUNDED
BY THE SOUNDS
OF SILENCE

PROTECTIVE.
A PLACE WHERE
I CAN BE WHO
I AM WITHOUT
SHAME

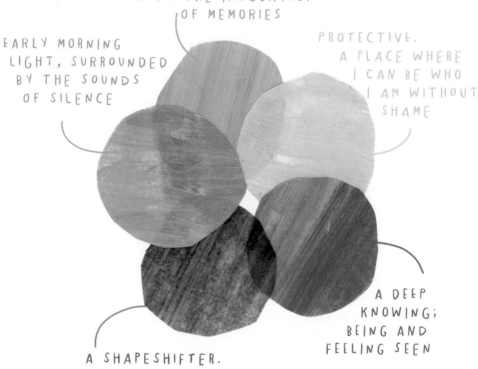

A DEEP
KNOWING;
BEING AND
FEELING SEEN

A SHAPESHIFTER.
HOME IS THE CORE OF
WHO I AM; IT CHANGES
AS I CHANGE & PROVIDES
WHAT I NEED WHEN
I NEED IT MOST

Home feels like trust: trusting that I will take care of myself, protect myself, and be there for myself when needed.

Home feels like peace: quieting the self-critical voice that tells me I am not enough.

Home is self-acceptance: welcoming myself and where I am in each moment, especially when I feel behind.

Home feels like grace: asking myself to do only what's possible in each moment and forgiving myself for all that I can't (or choose not to) do.

Home is loving myself: without the sincere practice of loving myself, self-trust and acceptance wouldn't be possible.

Identifying what feels (and doesn't feel) like home is fundamental to cultivating a sense of home wherever you go:

- When do you feel most at ease, free to be who you are without compromise?
- What people, places, or situations make you feel uncomfortable or evoke a sense of disconnection?
- When and where do you feel most understood?
- Which people and/or places reflect the characteristics and values most important to you, that you wish to cultivate within?

● ● ●

WHEN I THINK ABOUT LEAVING THE HOUSE

DID I TURN THE OVEN OFF? ARE THE DOORS LOCKED?

WHAT IF IT RAINS? WHAT IF I'M COLD? DO I HAVE A CLEAN MASK IN THE CAR?

WHAT IF SOMEONE HITS ME ON THE ROAD? WHAT IF I GET A FLAT TIRE?

WHAT IF IT ALL GOES PERFECTLY WELL?

WHAT IF THEY LOVE ME?

WHAT IF THEY DON'T LIKE ME? WHAT IF I SAY THE WRONG THING?

WHAT IF THIS DAY CHANGES THE COURSE OF MY LIFE?

I have a plethora of reasons for never leaving the house. These micro anxieties are each rooted in very real fears: the fear of being unprepared, the fear of rejection, the fear of death, the fear of being noticed, the fear of uncertainty. The more I indulge these fears, the stronger they grow. To be the person I want to be—someone propelled forward by interest, curiosity, and a sense of adventure—I've learned to quell these anxieties by examining my fears daily.

When I begin to feel anxious about leaving the house, I take a deep breath and pay attention to the voices in my head. I ask myself:

- What is making me feel anxious?
- What fear did this anxiety grow out of?
- What are the chances this fear will materialize?
- What actions will I take if it does happen?
- Will I be happier (and more fulfilled) if I stay home today, or if I push past this fear?

I'VE LEARNED to
QUELL MY ANXIETIES
BY EXAMINING MY
FEARS DAILY.

● ● ●

THE PLACES I TURNED TO WHEN I DIDN'T KNOW WHERE TO GO

THE WRITINGS OF
SEXTON, O'HARA,
YOGANANDA, HESSE,
AND NIN

THE STARS, SPARKLING
AND DANCING, FREE FROM
THE TRIVIALITIES OF
DAILY LIFE

EACH FRIEND WHO TOOK ME IN
WHEN I COULDN'T FIND MY WAY

OLDER VERSIONS OF MYSELF:
FINDING COMFORT AND
SAFETY IN KNOWING
I CAN ENDURE

THE MORNING AND NIGHT
SKY, BOTH OF WHICH
LISTENED & OFFERED
DIFFERENT PERSPECTIVES

What makes you feel cared for? Pay attention to the things that light you up—the conversations that help you feel understood, the art that eases you, the people you turn to without fear or embarrassment. These are the places you can turn to when nowhere feels safe.

Over the years, I've discovered where to go when I feel helpless: into solitude, where I can think, process, or enjoy the stillness of nothing; into books—the writings of Jericho Brown, Anne Sexton, or Hermann Hesse, which offer me new perspectives and companionship; toward friends who comfort me when I can't comfort myself; or to past versions of myself, who reassure me that this moment of uncertainty is merely a small dip in the line.

BEING HONEST WITH MYSELF IS THE hardest THING I'VE HAD to LEARN.

I work on letting go of the guilt I feel for needing or wanting help. I remind myself that asking for help is an indication of wisdom, not weakness. Being honest with myself is the hardest thing I've had to learn.

How did I discover where to turn? I asked myself the following:

- What do I need: discussion, direction, or simply to feel heard?

- What makes me feel most connected to myself and the world around me?

- Who makes me feel safe? Which people in my community regularly support me and offer objective, balanced advice?

● ● ●

WHERE I FOUND LOVE

ON A PARK BENCH
OUTSIDE OF
STARBUCKS
(AGE 15)

ON A GRASSY HILL
IN SUBURBIA
(AGE 19)

AT A FARM IN
DEERFIELD, IL (AGE 29)

IN A BASEMENT
APARTMENT IN BROOKLYN, NY,
WHEN I FIRST SAW MYSELF
(AGE 30)

ON A WINDING
TRAIL IN THE WOODS
IN NASHVILLE, TN
(AGE 30)

EACH TIME MY
CHILD LAUGHED
IN AN OLD BRICK
HOUSE IN ST. LOUIS, MO
(AGE 34)

t's April in Chicago, Illinois, still cold enough to require bundling before stepping outside. I lay out all the clothes in front of A—a shirt, a sweatshirt, sweatpants, socks, mittens, a scarf, hat, and boots. Today, we're going to the farm.

The animals mill about, ignoring the hands sticking through the wooden fence hoping to sneak a pat. A watches them carefully, noting the tails swishing and the large eyes blinking. He doesn't say much, but I see his mind moving. I know he's considering all he knows about them: that cows spend most of their day chewing, that they startle easily, that they don't usually like being alone.

We head over to the goats next, a restless bunch purposed for petting. A large crate of brushes stands in the corner solemnly. The pen is full of small children raking brushes through fur, while their grown-ups coax them, gently, to be gentler.

I urge A to pick up a brush, and after much hesitation, he does. He wanders over to a lone goat and combs him gently, being careful not to let the brush's plastic scrape against the goat's fur. He looks up at me and smiles.

The goat turns to A and sneezes—a rambunctious, floor-shaking goat sneeze that silences the entire pen. A bursts into tears. He runs toward me, his small, surprised body shaking with sobs. I am overcome with affection for this person who has been frightened by something he loves.

The bewildered eyes of my nephew—that's where I found love. Somewhere between the goats and the ride home, my tough edges were replaced with an oversized heart. I now have the fortune of finding love in all places, no matter how small, cold, or forgotten. Even the narrowest blade of grass glints with possibility.

●　●　●

THE PLACES I DON'T MISS

My tiny,
suburban childhood
town, where we were one
of few BIPOC families

MIDDLE SCHOOL,
WHERE BEING WELL
LIKED MEANT MAKING
SOMEONE ELSE FEEL
SMALL

THE CUBICLE
WHERE I WORKED FOR
EIGHT LONG YEARS

The room inside
my heart where
self—loathing
grows like ivy

THE CORNERS OF
MY HEAD THAT
REFUSE TO LET
ME BE...ME

The temples where I
was told to believe
without reason

There is a beautiful door inside my brain. It first appeared when I was fifteen, with a great, wallowing wave of despair I could no longer ignore. Maybe the door had always existed; I don't know—I didn't recognize it until I was already through it. Depression wasn't something I wanted to swim in; I simply was. I couldn't come up for air. I didn't know how to. Feelings of hopelessness and self-loathing cropped up each time I turned around. It was difficult to imagine a way out.

I wasn't depressed because I was ungrateful, willfully ignoring the immense amount of good in my life. It didn't develop because I was cynical or needed to think more positively—in fact, I practiced both gratitude and positive thinking regularly. I was depressed because a healthy mind requires certain connections: a meaningful connection to work, to community, and to a sense of purpose. These missing connections left me isolated. For a long time, until I first identified and later began building these connections, I felt very alone.

The door to my depression is a dark, mossy green. It is small and alluring. English ivy crawls over and through it, great big winding curls that fall away in wisps, cuffing any positive memory or feeling along the way. Whenever I pass it, I find myself looking back. Every few weeks, I stop right in front of it. I want to take a closer look, but I stop myself from getting too close. *No, thank you*, I say to myself. *I'm not going in there today.*

• • •

WHAT TO DO WHEN YOU COME TO A CROSSROADS

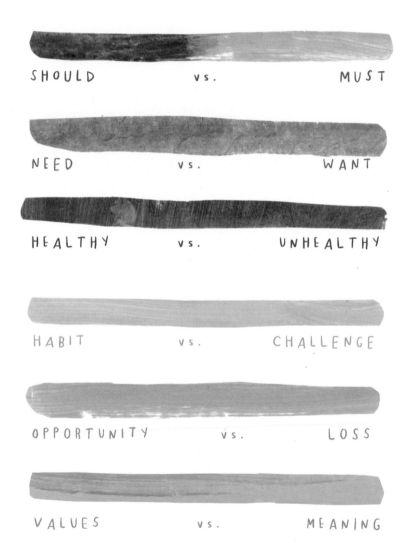

SHOULD   vs.   MUST

NEED   vs.   WANT

HEALTHY   vs.   UNHEALTHY

HABIT   vs.   CHALLENGE

OPPORTUNITY   vs.   LOSS

VALUES   vs.   MEANING

use the following questions to determine which road I should take:

- *Should vs. must?* Do I feel pulled toward this action internally or externally? Is this action self-affirming or fulfilling another person's expectations?

- *Need vs. want?* What am I hoping to obtain? Is it possible for me to achieve my goals without it?

- *Healthy vs. unhealthy?* Is this a healthy choice, or does it cater to the more impatient, indulgent parts of myself?

- *Habit vs. challenge?* Does this decision encourage my personal growth? Does it put me in a place of healthy discomfort or keep me from progression? Do I want to be safely stagnant or uncomfortably challenged?

- *Opportunity vs. loss?* What will I learn through this experience or decision? What do I risk losing?

- *Values vs. meaning?* Does this decision help me live in accordance with my values? Does it give my life meaning? Will I have greater purpose?

● ● ●

WHERE I WAS WHEN I FINALLY FELT LIKE MYSELF

ALONE

JOBLESS

FLOATING
FREELY

FULL
OF FEAR

WITHOUT
A HOME

've felt most like myself when I've deliberately introduced disruption into my life. There's so much weight inside a familiar routine: lazy habits, comfortable-but-uninteresting friendships, a lack of challenge. Starting over in a new city or stepping into a new life chapter requires me to lose my sense of security, but it's also freeing—it means I get to leave behind the rabble. Walking away is a privilege we're often unable to recognize and, therefore, unwilling to exercise. What feels like a jumble of confusion and a free fall into nowhere is really the best place I'll ever visit: it means I can start over. I am untethered and shapeless, free to become whoever feels most like me.

Of course, it isn't enough (and it won't always be possible) to create physical distance between myself and the people or places I feel stifled by. It's important to take ownership of my life by acknowledging that my mind is a large source of my own limitations. Eliminating my own idea of who I should be, little by little, sets me free.

ELIMINATING MY OWN IDEA of WHO I SHOULD BE, LITTLE BY LITTLE, SETS ME FREE.

• • •

HOW IT FEELS TO MOVE FAR AWAY FROM HOME

ANXIOUS.
Far from the people who know and love me, from the places that give me comfort and safety.

FREEING.
I can be who I am without a constant reminder of who I used to be.

OVERWHELMING.
New home, new city, new job, new relationships. No constant to ground me.

PROMISING.
A chance to start all over again.

CHALLENGING.
Exercising so many muscles that were comfortably dormant.

GRATIFYING.
The opportunity to depend on myself and be my own best friend.

I'd first been to Miami seven years ago when my sister lived here, having fallen in love with a man who moved her to Florida. I'd fallen in love with the clear water and intermittent storms, the way humidity made everything feel stagnant and temporary at the same time. Now, hundreds of miles away from my last home, not knowing where my next one is, I want to be somewhere familiar.

I find a spot on the beach that's fairly removed. I want to be near people, but not close enough for conversation. I practice feeling at home with where I am, which is alone.

I grew up in New Jersey and never moved anywhere farther than Philadelphia, Pennsylvania. For so long, comfort and familiarity were my priority because both ensured a feeling of safety. Staying in the same place meant I was able to retain many of my childhood friendships and community. It also meant constantly reshaping myself into the person they thought of me as, regardless of my inner evolution.

When I decided to travel alone throughout the country for a year, my anxiety rose like a wave. What would it feel like when I was all alone? What thoughts would haunt me when there was no one to distract me? What if I felt displaced everywhere I went? I left behind my home, family, friendships, and career—staples of the stability that had taken me my entire adult life to build.

In Miami, no one knows me. There are no reminders of the person I was or the places I've been. My past washes farther away from me with each receding wave, and the horizon stretches itself as far as the eye can see. There is nothing waiting for me here, or anywhere, and it's in this nothingness that freedom finds me.

● ○ ●

WHERE I FIRST LEARNED TO TAKE CARE OF MYSELF

PISCATAWAY, NJ—
THE OFFICE JOB
THAT FORCED ME
TO CHANGE MY
CIRCUMSTANCES

UNION SQUARE, NY—
WHERE MY THERAPIST
GENTLY EXCAVATED
THE BARRIERS THAT
STOOD BETWEEN MY
HEAD AND HEART

NEW BRUNSWICK, NJ—
ON NJ TRANSIT, COMMUTING
FROM SCHOOL TO WORK
AT 5a.m. WITH CARS
OF WEARY TRAVELERS

MIAMI, FL—
WHERE I LEARNED
TO KEEP MYSELF
SANE AND SAFE
WITHIN MY
OWN MIND

NASHVILLE, TN—
IN MY RELATIONSHIP,
BY ASKING FOR
WHAT I NEEDED

LONDON, UK—
THE FIRST
TIME I TRAVELED
INTERNATIONALLY +
FELT THE GRAVITY
OF INDEPENDENCE

On a blue winter morning in the middle of October, my friend K told me her Post-it story: after a particularly tough year, she stuck a Post-it on her mirror that said, "The fascination of the unknown is behind every corner," reminding herself that at any moment in time, everything can change—even if that change is beyond her visual periphery.

I was feeling stuck, so I thought I'd try her method. After all, anything is worth trying once or twice. On a small, turquoise square of paper I found somewhere underneath my bed, fallen from the pages of a secondhand book, it was written: "Everything is impossible until it works." Perfect. I stuck it on my mirror and brushed my teeth in front of it twice a day for about six months. Sometimes I flossed, and it flossed with me. It stared at me while I put on mascara or thought some thoughts. I painted it one morning when it felt like nothing was working and then hung it above my drafting table. It stayed solidly pinned, encouragingly, while I drew the outlines for books I hoped to write one day.

Since then, I've traveled to a lot of places. I took my nephews to school in Chicago, lay on beaches in Miami, remained a wizard in Orlando, listened to jazz in New Orleans, found everything in Nashville, climbed mountains in Zion National Park, saw the colors of Antelope Canyon in Arizona, and ate all the tacos in Los Angeles. In Kyoto, I heard the rustle of ancient bamboo trees talking to themselves, and I made a vow to listen to myself more.

I've met a lot of people and made a lot of memories, and even when I'm not sure where I'm going next, something inside me tells me I'll always be taken care of.

● ● ●

FINDING HOME
INSIDE MYSELF

ACCEPTING
MYSELF

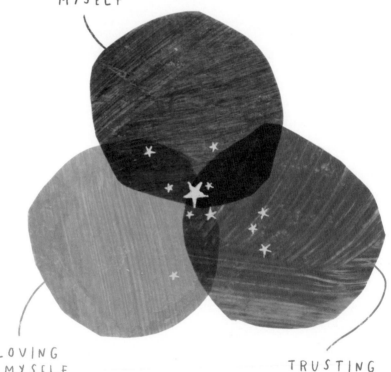

LOVING
MYSELF

TRUSTING
MYSELF

*I*t is 2016. I live in the basement of a two-bedroom Brooklyn apartment where sunlight streams in through the oblong windows. It's late afternoon, and the light is warm, dancing against the walls. If I squint my eyes, I can pretend I am anywhere.

It is 2018. I live on a small farm north of Nashville. The greenery is overwhelming, every shade imaginable in front of me: lime, emerald, mint, forest. The cicadas are loud and beat against my eardrums when I am trying to sleep. I wonder if I'll ever be anywhere else. So often it feels like time continues while I stand completely still, wondering who to become.

It is 2021. Like the rest of the world, I've cocooned myself entirely indoors, not having stepped off the farm in almost two years. In that time, I carried and birthed a small child named after every river. There is no time to think, to have any idea at all about who I now am. We spend all of May and June packing the memories of our young family into boxes and then we move to a new city altogether. We leave it all behind: the animals, the land, the home where our river was born.

In this new city, in a state I've never been to, I don't know anyone. Everything I own is in boxes in the center of each room, the belongings inside them forgotten. The sidewalks stretch in every direction, and at night I hear the traffic stream through my windows. There is so much to undo.

I've had to find my way back to the home inside me many times; each day I wake as someone new. I am lost in the depths of my own sea, swimming ceaselessly against the current. Sunlight dances against the innumerable paths before me, but it doesn't matter which one I take. Eventually, each one leads back to me.

● ● ●

FINDING
MY PURPOSE

FINDING
HOME

FINDING
FAMILY

FINDING
MYSELF

FINDING
LOVE

FINDING
FRIENDSHIP

THE PROCESS

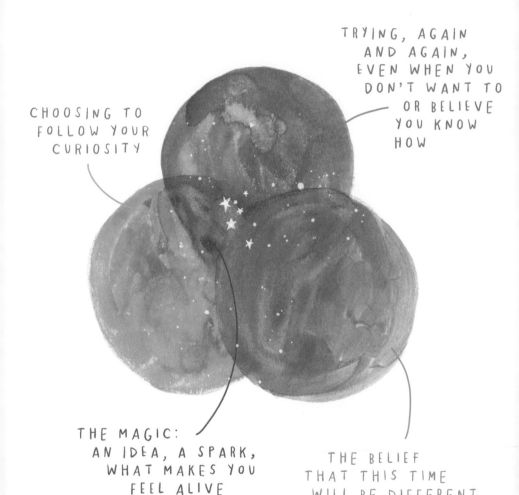

TRYING, AGAIN
AND AGAIN,
EVEN WHEN YOU
DON'T WANT TO
OR BELIEVE
YOU KNOW
HOW

CHOOSING TO
FOLLOW YOUR
CURIOSITY

THE MAGIC:
AN IDEA, A SPARK,
WHAT MAKES YOU
FEEL ALIVE

THE BELIEF
THAT THIS TIME
WILL BE DIFFERENT

I t's not the beginning or the end that matters. It's the middle bit, the part we struggle through—that's where our senses awaken and become alert, where we feel most alive. As an artist, I strive to create environments that step off the page, enveloping the viewer with color and feeling. The path toward this goal is littered with failure, terrible work, and self-doubt—none of which I'm particularly interested in experiencing. But it's during this process of trying that I find validation and surprise.

For the past week, I've been painting a portrait. I'm not very good at drawing people. I stop myself from trying often, too preoccupied with staving off failure and because it's discomforting to watch myself struggle. I don't know how to preserve someone's likeness in pencil and ink. How can I paint hope in their eyes? Or show that, like me, they're simply trying to find their way?

I'm about two months into graduate school, and all I've made is garbage. The good news is, I think that's what I'm supposed to be doing. The good news is, I think I'm in the right place. The good news is, I care a little bit less and try a little bit more. My painting is too large to frame, and the only part of it I like is a tiny bunny sitting in the corner. The good news is, I found something to like, someone to smile for. She sits, waiting.

I sit and wait, too, knowing it doesn't matter if the painting is good or bad. What matters is that I begin, that I try, and that I keep going.

● ● ●

WHAT AM I HERE FOR?

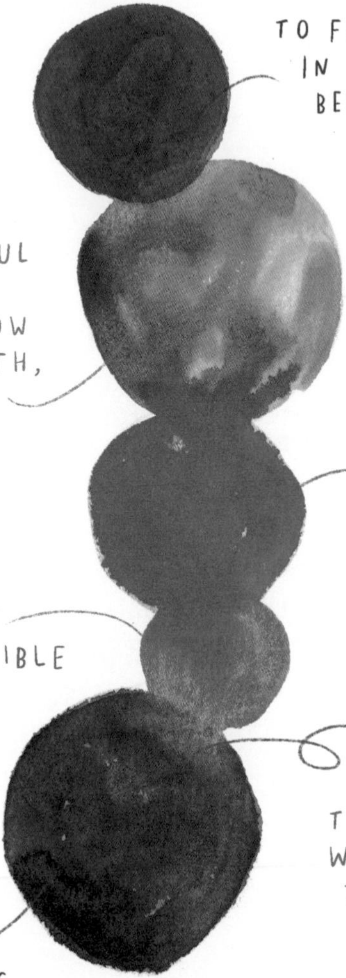

TO FIND GRATITUDE
IN WHAT LIES
BEFORE ME

TO TURN MUNDANE
TASKS INTO MINDFUL
MEDITATION:
A CHANCE TO SLOW
MY HEART, BREATH,
AND THOUGHTS

TO MOVE MY BODY
AND MARVEL AT
THE WONDER
OF IT

TO REMEMBER THAT
ANYTHING IS POSSIBLE

TO KNOW THAT
WITHOUT TEDIUM,
THERE IS NO
EXCITEMENT

TO REMEMBER
THAT LIFE
COMES IN WAVES,
AND THAT CHANGE
IS COMING, TOO

*I*t's 4:30 a.m., and I shuffle out of bed, rubbing sleep from my eyes. It feels too soon; it always feels too soon. The bathroom light is blinding so I brush my teeth in the dark, eyes closed, pretending I'm not awake and another day doesn't stretch before me. What will it ask of me today? That I give my best to all who ask for it? That I practice patience? That I try harder than yesterday? That I tire less easily? I try not to feel resentful as I shuffle down the stairs and through the narrow hallway toward the kitchen, passing my husband on the way. He's already made breakfast and let the dog out and now crawls around on all fours with the baby, roaring like a lion. His brilliant demeanor irritates me, but I make his coffee anyway—what else is there to do? Some people absorb love like a sponge and let it radiate from their faces like moonlight.

The baby waddles around, her teething mouth on everything—the stairs, the refrigerator, my shoes, the floor. I watch her intently, my face splitting into a smile.

What am I here for? To endure, I think, the best I can. To be present for it all—the husband, the child, the thunderstorm, and the occasional rainbow.

WHAT AM I HERE FOR? TO BE PRESENT FOR IT ALL.

● ● ●

WHEN I'M FEELING OVERWHELMED

I SHUT DOWN:
THERE ARE TOO MANY
EMOTIONS AND THOUGHTS
CYCLING THROUGH ME

AGITATION:
EVERYTHING IRRITATES ME,
HEIGHTENING MY ANXIETY

AWARENESS:
KNOWING THAT MY
ANXIETY IS SPINNING
AND I'M UNABLE
TO CALM IT

PARALYSIS:
INABILITY TO
PROCESS
WHAT I'M
THINKING
OR FEELING

REJECTING:
EVERYTHING,
INCLUDING
PEOPLE
AND ACTIONS
THAT CAN HELP

I find it helpful to deliberately identify and sort the feelings mishmashed inside me. I make a list of my responsibilities and then prioritize them in order of importance. This exercise enables me to eliminate or spend less time on tasks of little value, which take up most of my energy. I can then refocus, prioritizing the responsibilities and people I truly care about—including myself.

When you feel overwhelmed, try this:

Write it all down.

Answer the following questions:

- What's causing me anxiety?
- What are all the things on my to-do list?
- What do I feel guilty about?
- What do I wish I had, or could do, in this moment?

Transferring all the noise in your head onto paper enables you to see *why* you're overwhelmed. It becomes possible to quiet the sources of your overwhelm only after you've identified them.

● ● ●

WHEN I CHANGE
MY PERSPECTIVE

CREATING THE SPACE
NECESSARY FOR SURPRISE

GIVING OTHERS
THE CHANCE TO
CHANGE

GIVING MYSELF
THE OPPORTUNITY
TO BE WRONG —
TO LEARN
AND GROW

SETTING
INTENTIONS
INSTEAD OF
EXPECTATIONS:
TAKING BACK
RESPONSIBILITY
& CONTROL

MY FOCUS
RETURNS TO
THE WHY
(MEANING) RATHER
THAN THE OUTCOME
(EXPECTATION);
DISAPPOINTMENT
DISSIPATES

I'm agitated, disappointed in myself. I thought I'd be farther along by now. I need to send my final illustrations to the client by this evening, but I'm still working on the first round of sketches. The day is mapped out between day care pick-ups and drop-offs, graduate school classes, my job, and house chores. I have an exact amount of time slotted for each task; this is how I ensure everything gets done.

My expectations crowd me. They squeeze the life out of everything I do, making it impossible for me to be present. I focus on expectations ("Creating paintings that others will adore!" "I will be happy if I stick to my rigid schedule during these unprecedented times!") that I have little control over. Expectations are unforgiving; they reduce our feelings of ease and imagination—two ingredients necessary for thriving creativity. It's difficult to draw well with my brain in a vise, jammed between an increasingly long to-do list and a timer waiting to go off.

I decide to replace my expectations with intentions. I can't control what happens, but I can choose how I want to feel, and quite frankly, I'm tired of feeling disappointment each day. I say it aloud: "I intend to create work that meets others where they are. I intend to try my best with the time and limits I have. I intend to be kinder to myself."

I try this for a week and notice small shifts within. I'm able to recognize my progress and feel good about it, rather than obsessing over all I haven't achieved. I feel calmer and in control. I'm less reliant on external circumstances for satisfaction or fulfillment, knowing that although I can't always control what happens, I can control my intentions—what I choose to see, feel, and give—and that is enough.

● ● ●

WHAT ACCEPTANCE FEELS LIKE

A PUZZLING
EQUATION THAT FINALLY
MAKES SENSE

AN ANCIENT TREE:
WISE, STEADY, &
PROTECTIVE

A MASS OF
CONFUSION
LIFTING,
LEAVING
CLARITY
IN ITS
PLACE

BLOOMING:
THE WAY A FLOWER
SLOWLY UNFOLDS AFTER
STRENGTHENING ITS
ROOTS FOR SO LONG

THE STILL
MOMENTS
BEFORE THE
SUN FINALLY
RISES

*T*he skin over my stomach doesn't simply cover the muscles beneath it—it pools, a collection of water that ripples when I move. The muscles beneath have separated completely, leaving a several-finger-sized indentation beneath the surface. For ten months, I carried a body inside of my own. I experienced the usual barrage of physical symptoms, accepting them as temporary obstacles to what I wanted most: a healthy child.

I didn't consider the fact that some changes would be permanent. Afterward, I felt too foolish to admit it—did I genuinely believe my body could host another living thing without ramification? The guilt encouraged shame to settle deep within. I hated the way I felt. How unreasonable I was—how selfish, even—to expect my muscles to rejoin. I have a healthy child. *This is what I wanted.* How greedy I am to want my body, too.

For eight months, I tried to accept my body. *Be grateful*, I reminded myself. I couldn't accept that I was grateful *and* unhappy with my body. That I was grateful *and* physically weaker than before. That I was grateful *and* unable to recognize myself.

I began physical therapy and took daily walks with my family. I couldn't wear most of my wardrobe, but I separated the clothes I felt good in and put the others away. I developed an influx of energy, later realizing that I was no longer spending it hating my body.

I still lift my shirt to stare at my stomach, but I no longer grimace. Instead, I feel neutral: This is a stomach. This is *my* stomach. This is what it looks like. Some days I feel grateful for it and this body, which has done so much for me; other days I feel nothing at all. That, too, is enough.

● ● ●

WHAT DO I BELIEVE IN?

I FEEL INSIGNIFICANT—
WHICH OFFERS RELIEF

MY PERSPECTIVE
REBALANCES

A SENSE OF
AWE

I BECOME
MORE CURIOUS

ENERGIZED BY AN
EVER-REPLENISHED
WELL OF POTENTIAL

CALM

I'm part of a beautiful, complex universe whose significance stretches beyond my individual life. This thought grounds me when life feels overwhelming. It helps me cope with the trivialities of daily life so I can prioritize what brings me purpose: being more patient than I was yesterday, taking care of the community I live in, helping the people in my life feel supported.

I'm mesmerized by my own ability to breathe—to have a body that knows how to do it without instruction. To have eyes that automatically translate light and color into recognizable images for my brain. To feel the air on my skin. There is so much I don't understand. Magnifying these invisible wonders reminds me that life is a magnificent adventure. Remembering this, especially when life is difficult or messy, offers a real magic—the ability to find meaning in each of my days.

Discovering what you believe in is essential for creating a value system to live by. This system is flexible; it can—and should—change as you do.

As you begin exploring your beliefs, consider the following questions:

- What is my place in this world?

- How do I want to connect to the people, plant life, and animals I share this space with?

- What philosophies, if any, make sense to me? Which give me a sense of meaning and purpose?

- If I didn't worry about money or what other people thought of me, how would I spend my time?

● ● ●

AM I LIVING BY MY VALUES?

CURIOSITY:
about myself,
others, & the world

ASKING
QUESTIONS &
LISTENING

INDEPENDENCE:
self—reliant,
critical thinking

COURAGE:
the ability
to persevere

HONESTY:
with myself and others.
A gateway to
meaningful work
& relationships

CHOOSING TO
TRY AGAIN

CREATIVITY:
in how I approach
problem—solving &
my mental well—being

SELF—REALIZATION:
knowing who I am, which
allows me to live honestly

RESPECT:
for myself and others, which
leads to an open, kind heart

*T*wo types of motivation subconsciously guide us: internal motivation, which holds personal meaning and significance for us, and external motivation, which encourages us to act in the hopes of earning validation or acknowledgment from someone or something outside ourselves.

External motivation can be helpful, but it lacks the longevity and resilience that internal motivation cultivates. In my own life, I create art that urges self-exploration. If I were externally motivated—say, by the desire to win illustration awards or land on best seller lists—I'd run the risk of being resentful (if it never happens) or insatiable (if it does). I'd also eventually tire, because creating work that helps others is difficult. It requires me to regularly introspect, empathize deeply with others, and chronicle my vulnerability for the entire world. In addition, I carry the ache of those who encounter my work and wish to share their difficulties with me.

I spend time examining, and shifting, my values so my life follows a path of purpose. In doing so, I've discovered I'm internally motivated by a desire to help others through my work. Because I've explicitly outlined my core values, my internal compass points me toward them, especially when I feel tired or discouraged. Knowing that I am living harmoniously—that my actions and behavior are synced with my thoughts, values, and beliefs—inspires me to keep going. Simply put, living according to my values allows me to endure.

Questions to consider:

- What are my priorities and why?
- Are my goals internally or externally motivated?
- What people, places, and experiences feel meaningful to me?
- What qualities do I look for and admire in others?
- What values do I wish to cultivate within myself?

● ● ●

SHOULD I BE DOING MORE?

DOING
NOTHING

DOING
EVERYTHING

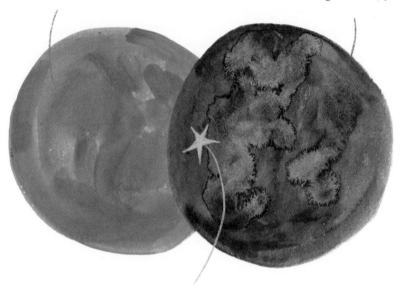

KNOWING I CAN
MAKE A DIFFERENCE

*T*here were no trash or recycling services when we lived on the farm—it was, after all, a farm. This was inconvenient, but it gave us the chance to be intentional about our waste. It made us more conscious of what we consumed and how we disposed of it after. We set up a composting system in the backyard where we turned our food scraps into rich, fertile soil. We separated our recycling into cardboard, plastics, glass, and metals and drove carloads to the local recycling center every two weeks. We ordered less online, more conscious about our purchases and the packaging they arrived in.

The problems of our time are overwhelming—so much so that a paralysis can set in. Unfortunately, paralysis is just that: paralysis. It doesn't encourage you to create change in yourself or the world, and it doesn't allow you to help anyone else. To break free, consider the following:

- *Helplessness stems from inaction.* Commit to fostering hope within yourself by believing that your actions matter—that there is meaning in every small deed, even if it seems underwhelming. Does it feel like enough? Never. Is it better than doing nothing at all? Yes.

- *Operating in a state of total despair (or, worse, being unable to function) doesn't mean you see reality more clearly than those who are content.* Cultivating joy within yourself despite the realities that surround you is a strength.

- *Ask yourself which causes align with your values.* Choose a single issue that is close to your heart. Learn more about it, and slowly integrate small changes in your lifestyle that support that cause.

- *Learn to live with fear and anxiety.* Remember that the presence of both indicates that you care—that you're a thoughtful, feeling person who wants to make a difference.

● ● ●

WHEN I THINK ABOUT WHAT HAPPENS AFTER

WHAT
I KNOW

POSSIBILITY

WHAT
I DON'T KNOW

Our home was built in 1905. The foundation has shifted considerably in the hundred years since; the floor of my studio slopes downward so badly that each piece of furniture is supported, and leveled, by shims. I lost many pencils to the recessed area beneath the radiator before I finally invested in a rug. My chair can't be leveled, so each time I sit down, life thrusts me forward, pushing me into the future. The days are long, but the months melt away too fast.

The walls are thick. Nearly a foot of brick and plaster comprises each one, making it impossible to drill a hole. My paintings are stacked on the floor. They've given up on their dream of being hung up and admired and instead collect dust, cobwebs, and my frustration each time I trip over them.

I'm standing in the living room, which is empty, trying to imagine what it should feel like. What kind of furniture does this home need? How should I arrange it? How long will we even live here? What will become of this home when we leave? And finally: What's the point?

I don't know, which is a relief, because it shatters the burden of having to know. I don't know, which is a freedom, because it allows me to imagine the possibility. I don't know, which is a balm, because it's only in a place of not knowing that I can heal.

I lie down on the bare floor. The wooden floorboards are scratched and discolored. A hundred years' worth of feet—some tiny and unsure, some not—have jumped, skipped, and sprinted across them. The windows are open, and dust dances within each sunbeam that wanders in. It floats along, without knowing how. And so do I.

● ○ ●

HOW TO KEEP GOING

ACCEPT LIFE'S
DUALITY

FIND
MEANING IN
THE DIFFICULT
& JOYFUL

BEGIN
AGAIN

MAKE
PEACE
WITH
CHANGE

KEEP
WHAT'S
USEFUL,
DISCARD
THE REST

LET GO
OF "SHOULD"

_T_hese days are short on grace, short on patience, short on sleep. Nobody gets the best version of me—she's buried under heightened anxiety, to-do lists, and the dull persistence of isolation.

It is difficult to admit that I am tired. Not long ago, I felt energized—confident enough to receive the unknown. But the past two years have hollowed me out. My pockets are empty, waiting to be filled. _How do we keep going?_ I don't know how to explain this thing that we're all trying so hard to do.

I do know how to take a walk, though, so I bundle myself up each morning and head outside. The frozen air smacks me in the face as I trudge through the snow, and the baby begins to wail in her stroller. I grimace and let the wind fill my ears instead; I keep going. After fifteen minutes, my revived heart is thumping furiously, and my limbs are awake. The baby has fallen asleep, her deep breaths now serving as my quiet soundtrack. It feels good to do this for myself.

Above me, a flock of birds cuts through the sky, moving in rhythmic patterns. I watch their trail, wondering if I'll ever feel like I know where I'm going. A single starling circles over me, adding twigs and straw wrappers to her nest. Each time the wind undoes her work, she patiently rebuilds her collection, poking leaves back into place. I watch her work tirelessly, admiring her determination. Her song is slow and sweet. Her movements are steady. The one thing this starling teaches me is the one thing I already know. In life and love and art and parenting, you can't really plan on it being good. The only thing you can plan on—all you can really count on—is whether you keep going.

When I get home, I call my sister. "I'm tired," I say. "I know," she says. "Me, too." We gripe about small things and big ones, we laugh in the face of it all, and when we hang up, I feel a little better. I find my husband and child in

HOW DO YOU KEEP GOING?

TURN YOUR FACE TOWARD THE SUN & RAIN; SEARCH FOR MEANING IN BOTH. IF YOU LOOK FOR IT, IT'S ALWAYS THERE. LET GO OF "SHOULD." MAKE PEACE WITH CHANGE. REST AS NEEDED— AND THEN, BEGIN AGAIN.

front of the record player, dancing wildly. We gather into a group hug and collapse onto the floor in a heap. N's wild hands keep waving, a tiny lighthouse guiding a lost ship home.

In the afternoon, we troop outside once again. N and T have busied themselves with bird-watching; a group of mourning doves sits on our backyard fence, hopping from post to post. I find myself listening to their conversations, both father-to-child and bird-to-bird. My heart begins to thaw. Everything softens in the open air. I stomp around the backyard, making huge cracks in the melting ice. Each loud *snap* brings more satisfaction than anything I've written or drawn in weeks. Sun filters through the bare branches. It all sharpens: my eyes, my mind, my will.

There are tiny movements behind me. I see N dodging pockets of snow, running wildly toward the dog. Her arms are open wide, ready for throwing around him. She hugs him gently, like we taught her to, and then steps back, laughing with delight. Like me, she begins to stomp around the backyard. Unlike me, there are no borderlines dividing the affection she feels for herself. I watch as both of her arms wrap around her own small body. With every stomp, she rocks back and forth, gently hugging herself closer.

A cold morning walk, a conversation with a loved one, a messy group hug, and affection for oneself—these small tokens form a bigger gift: renewed resilience against larger despair. Most days, I can consider heavier concerns without letting them swallow me whole. I can breathe. I find hope, however intermittently, in the tiny treasures within each day.

How do you keep going? Turn your face toward the sun and rain; search for meaning in both. If you look for it, it's always there. Let go of "should." Make peace with change. Rest as needed. And then: begin again.

●　●　●

Finding Yourself: The Beginning

*T*he following pages contain six blank palettes for you to color and caption. These palettes are a place for you to identify what matters to you now, in this moment, right where you are. Each palette serves as a starting point, a foundation where you can begin to define the values and boundaries that will help you build the sense of self, support, and purpose that are uniquely yours.

Over time, you'll find yourself changing. This is a natural response to life's push and pull; it indicates growth. When this happens, I encourage you to create new palettes that will serve the new person you are and the new places you'd like to go. When you tire or feel discouraged, I urge you to remember that you've done this work before—and to pull closer the strength that brought you this far.

● ● ●

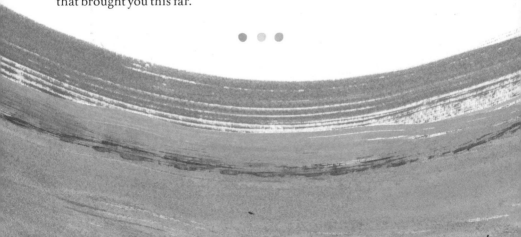

FINDING MYSELF

Fill the palette below with the qualities
you'd most like to cultivate within yourself.

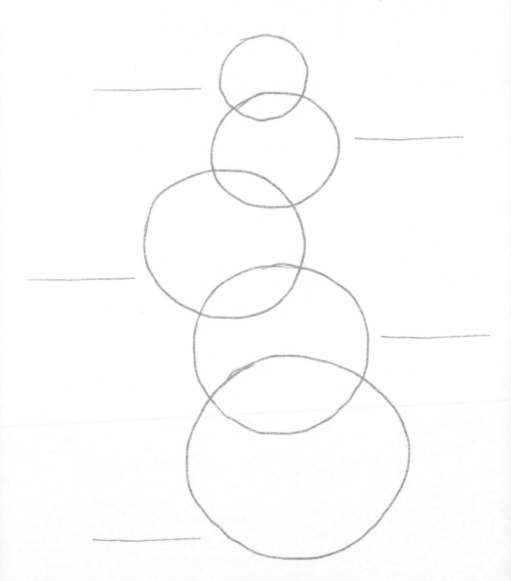

FINDING LOVE

What does healthy, supportive love feel like?

FINDING FRIENDSHIP

In what ways can you be a better friend?

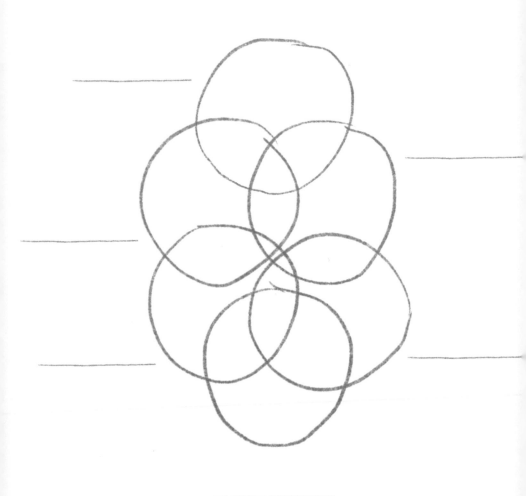

FINDING FAMILY

Who is in your chosen family?

FINDING HOME

What do you want home to feel like?

○
_____
_____

○
_____
_____

○
_____
_____

○
_____
_____

○
_____
_____

○
_____
_____

FINDING MY PURPOSE

What values do you wish to live by?

Acknowledgments

My deepest gratitude to the following people who made writing this book possible:

My partner, Trevor, who created time for me to write, even when there wasn't any—and for loving and supporting our little family throughout; my parents, who cared for us all; Jessica and Kristen, for your honest edits, comradery, and friendship; Laurie, for your enthusiasm and perspective on both writing and motherhood; and Marian, for your continued support and encouragement.

Lastly, to Nadi Luna, who stayed with me this entire time: we wrote these words together.

● ● ●

About the Author

Meera Lee Patel is a self-taught artist and author of several books on mental and emotional health, including the internationally bestselling *Start Where You Are: A Journal for Self-Exploration* and *My Friend Fear: Finding Magic in the Unknown.* Her books and journals have sold more than a million copies worldwide and have been translated into more than a dozen languages.

She lives with her family in St. Louis, Missouri. For more about Meera and her work, please visit meeralee.com or find her online @meeraleepatel.

● ● ●

ALSO BY

Meera Lee Patel

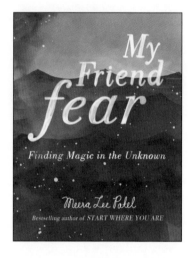

MEERALEE.COM